UNIVERSITIES
AND
REFLEXIVE
MODERNITY

UNIVERSITIES
AND
REFLEXIVE
MODERNITY

Institutional Ambiguities and Unintended Consequences

LAZĂR VLĂSCEANU

Central European University Press
Budapest–New York

© 2010 by Lazăr Vlăsceanu

Published in 2010 by
Central European University Press

An imprint of the
Central European University Share Company
Nádor utca 11, H-1051 Budapest, Hungary
Tel: +36-1-327-3138 or 327-3000
Fax: +36-1-327-3183
E-mail: ceupress@ceu.hu
Website: www.ceupress.com

400 West 59th Street, New York NY 10019, USA
Tel: +1-212-547-6932
Fax: +1-646-557-2416
E-mail: mgreenwald@sorosny.org

ISBN 978-963-9776-49-4 paperback

Library of Congress Cataloging-in-Publication Data

Vlăsceanu, Lazăr.
  Universities and reflexive modernity : institutional ambiguities and
unintended consequences / Lazăr Vlăsceanu.
     p. cm.
  Includes index.
  ISBN 978-9639776494 (paperback)
  1. Education, Higher--Europe. 2. Educational change--Europe.
  3. Universities and colleges--Europe. 4. Civilization, Modern I. Title.
  LA628.V63 2010
  378.4--dc22
                                                          2009036859

Printed in Hungary by
Akadémiai Nyomda, Martonvásár

Table of Contents

List of Tables

Acknowledgments

This book developed out of an in-depth reflection on modernity and its recent impact on the university. Without having extensive conversations and exchange of ideas with my colleagues in UNESCO–CEPES and with those from various European universities and organizations, its contents would have probably been different.

Special thanks are to be addressed to those with whom I closely co-operated in finalizing some of the chapters. The one on "Demography and Higher Education," which was part of a UNESCO–CEPES project, was drafted with the constant and imaginative inputs and support of Laura Grünberg. "The New World of Higher Education" was initially published in Romanian as part of a volume on "Sociology and Modernity. Transitions towards Reflexive Modernity" (Polirom, 2007). It was translated from Romanian by Cecilia Preda, and Peter Wells turned Romanian English into the English of a Romanian.

Many thanks are addressed to Mariana Gherman and Carmen Donciu who constantly helped me understand how many personal imperfections may be compensated by someone so close to my work. The final version of the publication came out only after Professor Marvin Lazerson looked closely at the whole manuscript. He raised so many interesting questions and formulated such comments and suggestions that made me think not only about a particular text but also about some future projects which may better respond to his expectation.

Introduction

Once published, a book has the fate of solitude: it often ends up isolated in solitary reading and then on a bookshelf, its history forgotten, and most of its generating links, including those with the author, virtually ignored. Any book, though, is part of the professional and intellectual path of the author, a sort of provisional outcome of an endless chain of experiences, hypothesizes and ideas. It has a history of its own, which is inextricably entangled with that of the author. Yet the author is rarely prepared to reveal such a history, leaving it to an interpretation based on a world of implicit understanding and speculation. With this volume I would like to take a different stand, and reveal some of those implicit meanings associated with my personal history.

The events, specifically the anti-communist revolution which began in December 1989 and the ensuing long period of transition in Romania, have seen students and universities as front-runners of change. Both proved then and now to be the most radical actors, ready to transform the world of the past and bring about a new order of things in all realms of life and society, including that of their universities. At that time, when almost every action and/or change was possible and necessary, I found myself confronted with many responsibilities, firstly at the University of Bucharest and subsequently at the national level of the higher education system. It so happened that, almost overnight, from the position of a junior lecturer I was elected and pushed by various events to assume, together with other colleagues, the tasks of reforming higher education institutions and the system as a whole. Due to the role of students in those revolutionary days, universities also appeared as important forces for changing and reforming society as a whole. Such a romantic ethos and places of action were both cultural and political and more often than not were constantly expanding. A breakthrough came about for me on this journey. I found that politics, which at the time spread so rapidly that it invaded all aspects of life, including personal ones, did not match my way of being, because I did not sit comfortably in its chaotic configurations. When the opportunity arose, I left the university and joined a global organization, UNESCO, which happened to have a decentralized office in Bucharest (i.e., Centre européen pour l'enseignement supérieur—or CEPES for short).

After joining UNESCO–CEPES, I lived concomitantly in two worlds, which only occasionally met each other. There was the global stage of UNESCO and higher education, which carried me from San José to Moscow, from Jerusalem to Dubrovnik, from Madrid and Paris to Tokyo and Washington. There was also the World Bank and the Council of Europe, the European University Association and the Open Society Institute, a whole range of intergovernmental and nongovernmental organizations with programs in higher education. In all this there was constantly a strong personal involvement in launching, implementing and evaluating higher education projects in Romania and elsewhere. I was thus in and out of my Romanian university: twin perspectives which more often than not quarreled with each other when they did not manage to be complementary.

Having now such an experience and reaching the stage

of distancing myself from UNESCO, I thought that the time is ripe to write a book about the challenges and uncertainties facing today's university. I leave it to the reader to see how many of the uncertainties are those of the author and which are institutional uncertainties. Of one thing I am clear: institutional and personal histories do meet and sometimes converge allowing, when possible, for routes to changes and/or conservation.

This book is then a chronicle of recent and current changes in the university. In doing so, certain references are of key importance. The first one is indeed personal. Most of my professional life has been related to and spent in universities, either as an insider who played various teaching and research roles or as an outsider with national, regional and even global managerial experiences. I have had numerous opportunities and chances to move in and out of the university, to combine and single out views, to construct and deconstruct them as the time went by. In so doing, I could see how the old university has strived to preserve its traditional *raison d'être* and also how it has had to change in order to cope with various uncertainties of our time. When reflecting on how the university could better cope with contemporary challenges, history has stepped in and made me enter reflexively into the world of modernity. After all, our modern university was shaped by the twin pillars of modern thought: modern philosophy, with its method of reflection initiated by René Descartes, and modern science, with the rationality which Isaac Newton put forward in physics and which irradiated to many other domains of human endeavor.

History tells us that, since the dawn of modernity to now, the transformations have been dramatic. For some, indeed for many, upon reaching the beginning of the 21st century two alternatives opened up: either modernity lost its legitimacy and thus we enter an age of post-modernity, or we are confronted on a large scale and for the first time with the products generated by modernity itself. Sociologists like Anthony Giddens[1] or Ulrich Beck[2] have thoroughly reflected on such an issue. I, like many others in the same vein, find that the prefix "post," so much in use when referring to our times, does not tell us anything more than signaling a difference between the present and the past. The idea of modernity coming to an end and of post-modernity taking shape in all life-worlds is as dramatic as it is obscure: it is meant to mark off an identifiable period of history, with its beginnings and ends, but without really specifying those marks which would demonstrate that we have truly entered into a new era that is as different as would deserve a new name. The world of the modern university, with its past and actual configurations, may be brought in with its shades and lights and demonstrate convincingly that, far from leaving behind its traditional ways of being and functioning, it stretches them to their upper limits and demands wide reflexivity. It is only by becoming more reflexive that the university may better cope with the students' flow massification, the shrinking of public funding, the emerging academic markets, globalized academic fields, increased institutional autonomy and demanding stakeholder accountability. These were all initiated modestly by the dawn and then marching of modernity, and nowadays they are reaching the stage of new configurations and appropriately demanded policy making. Institutional risks are now multiplying; uncertainties facing institutions, students and staffs grow endlessly; calls for convergent actions across institutions and national systems take concrete forms, such as those encompassed in the European "Bologna Process" and the "Lisbon Accords."

Universities are by all accounts "temples" of science, that is of rational knowledge based on facts and experiments, on theory testing and fallibility. In terms of their structure and functioning, the foundation stones are of a different type, taking the form of a standard account based on general beliefs. These are nothing more but those received views of modernity labeled Humboldtian, Napoleonian, Oxbridgian or Anglo-Saxonian models of the university. Yet the existence of a consensus based on traditional beliefs, past models and dismissed options is one thing; their operational value in the newly emerging societal contexts, the soundness of that view, the validity and reliability of the historical assumptions on which it depends, are something else. There are many questions today that are sufficiently open to doubt and profoundly related to new developments, to justify our starting new enquiries, here and now, by looking freshly and more closely at the actual configurations and at their historical grounds, for providing the new standard account of the university today.[3] A new university is emerging. New "horizons of expectation," as Stephen Toulmin[4] would label them, call for reflection. Coming to terms with new "horizons of expectation" means, among other things, avoiding the opposition between the imagination of facing the future and the nostalgia of backing into it without any prospects. In what follows, an attempt to blend the two is modestly put forward in order eventually to stir more imaginative talents to better understand the future of the university in this time of high reflexive modernity.

When using the phrase "reflexive modernity," I rely entirely on that meaning which relates various attempts of modernizing the contemporary university with the knowledge or the systematic reflection on the options of that modernization process and on its uncertainties, challenges, risks and unintended consequences. In the first part, certain uncertainties and risks are identified and highlighted. In the second part, a more contextual perspective is put forward by confronting various options and scenarios when identifying models of modernizing the today's university and of relating it to processes of societal development. The key question here is that of distinguishing between universities that are "reflexive" and thus embarked on rapid processes of modernization and those which persevere on the traditional roads which they consider as being as safe as counter-modern. Reflexivity may be the answer and this book intends to contribute to its enhancing process.

August 2009, Bucharest   *Lazăr Vlăsceanu*

NOTES AND REFERENCES

1 Anthony Giddens, *The Consequences of Modernity*, Cambridge, Polity Press, 1990.

2 Ulrich Beck, *Democracy Without Enemies*, Cambridge, Polity Press, 1998. See also, by the same author: *Risk Society. Towards a New Modernity*, London, SAGE Publications, 2005 (firstly published in English in 1992).

3 However, history accounts differently in different countries. Take for instance France with its history of the university. Claude Allègre, former minister of education, research and technology in France, presents such an account by referring to the positions of students and teachers in various historical periods: "[...] *Toute l'histoire de l'Université française peut être résumée comme le résultat d'un antagonisme. D'un cote, la pression des autorités politiques pour remettre l'élève et donc la formation des élites (et donc l'intérêt national) au Cœur du dispositif. Et de l'autre, les tentatives de rejet successives du corps professoral pour s'y opposer. Les corps professoral n'a pas compris qu'il était l'élément*

essential, opératoire, mais pas la finalité de l'Université. C'est pour cette raison que la Révolution française supprimera l'Université, jugée corporatiste et réactionnaire. Pendant trois ans, il n'y aura plus d'universités en France. Elle créera à la place les grandes écoles. La, des leur fondation, les révolutionnaires placent l'élève au Cœur du système éducative. […] elle y place aussi comme sujets d'enseignements les nouveaux savoirs utiles; art de l'ingénieur, architecture, etc., que l'Université refuse obstinément d'enseigner. Pour ceux qui aiment les formules lapidaires, on pourrait dire que les grandes écoles c'est la République, l'Université c'est l'Ancien Régime." In: Claude Allègre, *Vous Avez Dit Matière Grise?*, Paris, Plon, 2006, p. 65.

4 Stephen Toulmin, *Cosmopolis. The Hidden Agenda of Modernity,* New York, The Free Press, 1990.

PART I

COPING WITH UNCERTAINTIES

CHAPTER 1

The Clash between Academic Traditions, Markets and GATS

1.1. INTRODUCTION

Two categories of developments may be distinguished in higher education today. One category refers to those developments which follow the traditional well-established academic patterns, while the other includes everything that is related to the emerging/existing markets in higher education. These two categories find their expression in distinctive discourses which, more often than not, seem to follow parallel tracks. Each one has its own concepts and expressive niceties; each is associated, in a more or less explicit way, with specific ideologies, which underpin certain varieties of academic action and organization. The free-trade model, more often associated with the higher education systems and institutions of USA, UK or Australia and the continental European protectionist model are not just different concepts, but organizational models that function differently in an increasingly globalized world of higher education.

However, some recent events together with their corresponding developments have troubled the parallelism and brought about a real clash between the two discourses. One such event was the adoption in Marrakesh in 1995 of the General Agreement on Trade in Services (GATS), which also refers to educational services. GATS started to have a greater impact on the

academic world four years later, at the conclusion of
the "Millennium Round" of multilateral trade negotiations, initiated by the World Trade Organization
(WTO) in Seattle in November 1999. This new market
discourse on higher education was thus formalized and
is also associated with specific commercial and legal
institutions, very different indeed from the ones traditionally operating in higher education. It comes as no
surprise that the new developments are regarded by
many academics as external and superimposed on
(higher) education and as inducing concepts and procedures which tend to be alien to the very nature of education and educational institutions.

The other instance that has helped in bringing about
the clash between the two dominant discourses on higher education is not by all means external to academe. It
takes the form of the growth of corporate, for-profit, private and virtual universities, all of them generating a
new and apparently unlimited institutional diversification in higher education. To complicate things even more,
many classical (conventional) universities have started
to promote those changes in their organization and
management which strengthen corporate operations
and identity, thus responding to market challenges. A
strong wave of "corporatization" of higher education
institutions, mainly through the use of new managerial
tools, is at work all over the world, even though the pace
may vary nationally or regionally. And these again are
developments which distance themselves from the traditional academic patterns, thus strengthening the market
approach to and discourses on higher education.

In such circumstances, the two categories of developments in higher education and their corresponding discourses are seen not only as parallel, but also as clash-

ing, thus affecting the stability, indeed, for many the survival, of the university as it has been so far known. A word like "crisis," so much used in the 1960s and 1970s, seems to be inappropriate today, when the academic world is invaded, and not just affected, by the market and its associates. Even some traditional educators seem to have been "catapulted" in front of the new waves of developments. Confronted with such a situation, their concerns were voiced by such an analyst as Kit Carson, who did not hesitate to say that "only a fool would deny the reality of the market; only an even greater fool would advance that discourse as the only language in which to debate our predicament."[1] The problem here, however, is not so much that of a discourse, than that of the reality to which that discourse is related. It is obviously impossible to deny a discourse while recognizing the reality to which it refers. For this reason, an analysis of the two types of developments and of their discourses is proposed in what follows. Higher education as an academic world versus its conception as a service world is examined closely, by confronting the approaches to higher education as a market or as a "public good," and by exploring this debate in regard to the GATS implications for trade in higher education and services.

The basic idea put forward is that the two types of development are neither parallel nor do they only clash; they co-exist as two paradigms which borrow from each other's approaches and developments those that best fit the momentous needs and concerns. The end result is a mixture of traditional and market practices and discourses.[2] Once losing its unitary traditional discourse and policy, higher education finds itself caught in a mixture of (contradictory) discourses, associated as they are with managerial actions and academic developments

which have lost their previous purity, being generated
by principles which belong either to the traditional code
of good action, or to the market code or to both at the
same time. It is in such a context that higher education,
and particularly the university, seems to lack today any
sense of historical perspective, acting mostly in a reac-
tive and momentous way, mixing up codes of action and
discourses which used to be separated. Such a mixture is
also clouded by the so-called boundary objects, which
belong to both categories at the same time. Where such
a situation may lead is a question for the future. Our
concern here is only that of bringing to the fore the mixture, indeed the clashing, of codes and paradigms and
their uncertainties, and of contextualizing them within
the framework of "reflexive modernity," a phrase I propose to use for describing further the current state of
affairs in higher education.

Indeed, when relating such developments to some of
the key meanings of "reflexive modernity," one may see
how the traditional disjunctive ways of looking at certain developments, such as that of the "either–or" type,
have been substituted by the conjunctive "and–and"
type of co-existence: *both* free market *and* protection-
ism, *both* trade *and* public good. The university of the
"First Modernity" was mostly related to the needs and
expectations of the nation-state, despite its uses of the
"universal science." How to ensure the production, transmission and reproduction of universal values of science
in order to meet national demands for highly specialized
workforce and technology was a key question for the
university of the first modernity. A combination of universality and of its specific confinement within the containers of the nation-state was the major challenge for

this university, since universality was restricted by the taken-for-granted assumption of national differences that demanded for well protecting fences. A new question has come about together with the second modernity: how tenable is such a development these days when finding itself confronted with the pressures of rapid economic and technological innovation within the framework of that global capitalism which is championed by the movement of neoliberals? The university is thus faced with the need of re-inventing itself and it does so by breaking down some of those old boundaries which were consecrated during the first modernity. This is far from being a smooth process. Contradictions, ambiguities and a wide range of uncertainties are at work. Ulrich Beck, referring to the world of work, describes brilliantly such a state, and *mutatis mutandis* may well be applied to the world of contemporary academe:

> The first modernity gave a series of institutionalized answers to the problems facing society: more and better technology, more and better scientific research, more and better functional differentiation. But these answers no longer convince us; they no longer engage with the situation. For contemporary societies are going through a fundamental transformation which radically challenges the understanding of modernity rooted in the European Enlightenment. The field of reference is now made up of many different options, and new, unexpected forms of the social and the political are emerging within this field.[3]

Let us explore further such developments.

1.2. TRIGGERING THE DEBATE

The debate on the clash between the traditional and the market paradigms in higher education was exemplified and intensified by the adoption of the General Agreement on Trade in Services in 1995. Since then, both negotiations, under the auspices of the World Trade Organization, for increasing international trade liberalization, and debates on, indeed protests against, the inclusion of "education" as a tradable service have taken place. Negotiations were resumed after the 1st of January 2000, and the Member States of WTO, acting in line with the provisions of GATS, further expected to broaden and deepen their liberalization commitments in order to increase the liberalization of trade in all service sectors. Following the decisions associated with GATS, two consequences have become obvious. One is that education in general and especially higher education are the concerns not only of academics and their institutions, but also of others, like, for instance, the ministries of trade and commerce, which used to be external to the academic world. On the other hand, a new discourse on higher education, as well as a new policy approach, has been institutionalized, the latter bearing upon the ways higher education is managed and practiced.

According to GATS and also following the United Nations Central Product Classification (CPC) System, the service sectors cover a wide range of services, from business, communication or transport services to tourism, health-related or financial services. Among the eleven basic services one sector refers to educational services. As in the case of any other service, four modes of trade in educational services are distinguished by

GATS: *cross-border supply* (the service itself, e.g., the study program, crosses the border); *consumption abroad* (a service consumer, e.g., a student, moves to another country to obtain the service); *commercial presence* (facilities established abroad by the service provider in partnership with a local organization, for instance under the form of a branch campus, for delivering a specific service); *presence of natural persons* (a person working temporarily in a country, different from that of his or her origin, to provide a service, e.g., a consultant, a visiting professor, etc.). This GATS classification refers, however, not only to the *modes of services trade*, but also to the *modes of delivering* or *supplying the services*. The two are then to be seen as interdependent, in the sense that when distinguishing modes of delivery one also prepares the grounds for regulating and evaluating levels and trends in trade in higher education. The two are also separate issues, in the sense that they are often dealt with by different instances for different purposes. For instance, considering educational services, one may insist, even exclusively, on the academic and pedagogical aspects of delivery, (i.e., modes of service supply), while the other, on the commercial implications and practices (i.e., modes of service trade). When the two are put together or they come closer together, various problems emerge that deserve further analysis. Consider for example two of the many questions that may be raised:

- How and why the modes of higher education service delivery were identified with the modes of services trade?
- What consequences are to be considered when higher education is seen from the perspective of trade liberalization?

Such questions have already been addressed in the debates focused on the implications of GATS.[4] Conferences, papers and even street demonstrations highlighted and sometimes obscured many of the issues of concern. When attempting to summarize all this, one may see how the answers put forward have come either from the traditional academic world or from the one focused on the workings of the higher education market. It is then necessary to confront these two worlds by exploring either their corresponding approaches or, indeed, their differences and contradictions.

1.3. HIGHER EDUCATION AS AN ACADEMIC AND/OR AS A SERVICE WORLD: THE PLACE OF "BOUNDARY OBJECTS"

Traditionally, and this tradition is centuries old, higher education and services production and trade have altogether been two separate worlds; the boundaries between them have been clearly drawn and protected; the historical narratives have followed different tracks and discourses, and their social roles and functions have rarely been set up as turning toward convergence.

On the one hand, higher education has been the world of that kind of academic work in which both the knowledge transmitter and the knowledge producer have been considered, and indeed have regarded themselves, as fully autonomous knowledge owners, invested with the academic freedom of carrying out their disinterested inquiries for the sake of furthering the knowledge and publishing the results without any fear of interference from a political, economic or administrative body. The ideal of the university has been that it should be regarded and protected, primarily in Europe, as a "public good." Mostly since the nineteenth century, even though the echoes go further back into history, universities have been regarded as acting as the intellectual consciousness of society, as nation-building institutions, as engines of social, economic and personal development, as depositories of the mostly praised cultural values and national heritage. Higher education has more or less received full public support, being considered as the forum of free debate, as the most effective producer of knowledge, as the promoter of new ideas and alternatives for development. Scholarship and citizenship, social mobility and leadership have been closely inter-related within the world of higher education. The public has constantly considered higher education as critical to society. No matter how much trust one may attach to such views, this dominant ideology was traditionally related to the university and one may encounter it even today in many academics' references.

On the other hand, the world of most services has belonged to or has been perceived as belonging to another realm, particularly to that of the economy. Most of its products and exchanges have been subject to trade on the market, to business operations, to a whole set of rules related to property rights and their protection.

These two traditionally separated worlds—higher education and services—are now intersecting to the extent that one (higher education) is submitted to the rules governing the other (services). The boundaries between the two are becoming troubled, in the sense that various "boundary objects," emerging from the blending of the higher education and the service sector, cluster together to generate a new mix of discourses and practices. The emerging narratives and practices are both academic and economic in order to account for the turning of higher education into a service and of the service into knowledge loaded trade.

Such "boundary objects," as the theory put forward by Joan Fujimura and Corynne McSherry states, carry with them certain ambiguities, which generate actual or latent tensions and many uncertainties. The theory goes further to mention that it is in the nature of such "boundary objects" to be "often ill-structured, that is, inconsistent, ambiguous, and even illogical."[5] They are invested with multiple meanings, and the discourses, indeed practices, using them may induce parallel tracks of development, but also a creative storm of explorations and interests as well as a preservation of the well established traditional practices in certain well hidden corners. The end result may possibly look like a mosaic of happenings and trends, which are sometimes contradictory and very often tense, unstable and contingent.

It is important to stress that "boundary objects" are context related. That is the context as such is generating what may be perceived as a "boundary object" or as a "pure object." In our case, the very mix of traditional and new developments and of their corresponding discourses generates "objects" which are taken over by one or the other at the same time, while contextualizing them in ways which are dramatically distorting. This makes them hardly recognizable when applying a perspective related to the real origin and reference of the "object" under consideration.

1.4. SEARCHING FOR
"BOUNDARY OBJECTS"

There is no doubt that discourses, indeed various policies and practices in the higher education of today are saturated by such "boundary objects." In what follows some of them will be outlined. However, it is necessary beforehand to explain why only higher education is being considered. Doing so is important because GATS encompasses all educational services—from primary and secondary education (that is "basic education") to higher education and adult education.

Basic education is almost universally considered as an item of "public consumption," being provided free of charge by governments. When considering the financial resources invested by governments in basic education for assuring its "public consumption" on an equal basis by all children of the corresponding age, and also the importance attached to education by all national authorities, in terms of its contribution to the formation of well educated citizens, it becomes self-evident that all governments want to retain full control over basic education. In a "background note" of the WTO Secretariat, mention is made of the fact that "basic education provided by the government may be considered to fall within the domain of, in the terminology of the GATS, services supplied in the exercise of governmental authority […]."[6]

The implication of the phrase "services supplied in the exercise of governmental authority" (Article 1.3. of the Agreement) is twofold. On the one hand, such services, like primary and secondary education are exempted from the GATS provisions, since they are both funded and provided by the government in the exercise of its authority. On the other hand, being so provided and funded, there would be no commercial or competitive alternative for providing the service. Conversely, when a service is provided on a commercial basis and in a competitive environment, "the exercise of governmental authority" is suspended and the GATS is applicable. This seems to be the case of higher education for some, though many others have formulated strong objections and have criticized such an approach.[7] It is then necessary to look more closely at higher education in order to identify the developments that have taken place there in such a way as to lead to its falling immediately under the jurisdiction of GATS provisions.

1.5. HIGHER EDUCATION BETWEEN MARKET AND "PUBLIC GOOD"

"Boundary objects" are context related and historically generated, in the sense that they correspond to a specific area of higher education and to a given academic space and time. They translate into concrete actions and symbolic expressions like certain codes, managerial patterns and incentives that belong concomitantly to both the traditional (i.e., first modernity) and the market (i.e., second modernity) higher education. For identifying such "boundary objects," let us consider higher education as a "public good" and as a market.

Higher education has been traditionally regarded as a "public good" for its contribution to the economic and social development of society, while also preserving, interpreting and further expanding the history and culture of a given society. Universities have been generously funded by governments. Students and graduates have been among the privileged élite of the societies. Since the nineteenth century, higher education institutions have been invited to leave their "ivory tower" and to provide services to communities. One could hardly anticipate that the service function of universities—one among other functions, and by no means a central one—would then turn into a key function, so that the whole of higher education could be itself identified as a service. And this change is not simply one of words. We are dealing here with a change of paradigm or, as P. Altbach put it, "we are in the midst of a true revolution in higher education, a revolution that has the potential to profoundly change our basic understanding of the role of the university."[8] It is in this changing process that "boundary objects" appear and generate uncertainties for some, and specific ways of acting for others.

Higher education as a "public good" may be considered from either an economic or a managerial (political) perspective. Regarding the latter, the emphasis is put on the regulatory role of governments and on their functions for providing means and defining public policies focused on the domain. Higher education appears as a "good," the production and distribution of which are provided under the responsibility of and with the funds offered by government, for the latter is democratically elected and legitimately empowered to design and implement those policies which serve the public. Academics are implicitly or explicitly regarded as "civil servants" to whom governments delegate the power of implementing the designed and approved public policies. Academics and their higher education institutions are provided with autonomy and freedom of action, but these are to be seen as relative to or limited by the public framework defined by the government in power.

An extensive literature in economics or policy analysis has been focused on the characteristics that distinguish public or collective goods from private or individual goods and this obviously bears on our topic here. Among others, Vincent Ostrom and Elinor Ostrom[9] considered two essential characteristics: exclusion ("when potential users can be denied goods or services unless they meet the terms and conditions of the vendor") and jointness of consumption (when consumption by one person does not preclude the use or consumption by another). These two characteristics are both independent and vary in degree in a dichotomous way: exclusion can be feasible or infeasible, and jointness of consumption may take the form of alternative or joint use. By arraying these defining characteristics in relation to one another, four logical types of goods have been revealed by the two authors: private goods (exclusion is feasible and the use is alternative), toll goods (exclusion is feasible and the use is of a joint type), common-pool resources (exclusion is infeasible and the use is alternative), public goods (exclusion is infeasible and the use is joint). Following on this classification, the result is that most governmental services are of the public good, toll good or common-pool resources types. Most importantly, the question is as follows: are educational services less of a public good type, taking instead the form of toll goods for which "user charges" are introduced as substitutes for taxation? When considering that only in some systems of higher education the mechanisms of "user charges" or of voucher systems have been introduced, it seems right to assume that higher education in Europe operates both as a public good (when the students are charged no fees) and as a toll good (when students pay tuition fees or a voucher system operates). The economic implications are different in the two cases. For instance, higher education as public good is mostly perceived as a free good, and the individual costs are not proportioned to the benefits. When higher education operates as a toll good, market mechanisms also intervene and those receiving the benefits of higher education pay, at least partially, for its costs. A principle of fiscal equivalence may also be at work here, choosing one alternative ("tax now") or the other ("tax later") with regard to the beneficiaries of higher education.

Further, from the traditional economic perspective such as that proposed by Paul A. Samuelson, when saying that higher education is a "public good," the meaning is that every unit of such a good that is produced is equally available for consumption by all.[10] The implication of this understanding would be that each student is provided with *equal* access to *publicly* supported higher education facilities. Such an understanding has had a long lasting career, even though it may be questioned in terms of both effectiveness of public organization and of efficiency of equal provision of public support to each student.

As a matter of fact, the benefits of education are not only personal, but also social, in the sense that many, if not all, types of education, while contributing to personal development, also have effects from which other persons, indeed families and communities at large, benefit. The external effects of education are obvious: in a community with a larger proportion of highly educated people, everyone belonging to that community will benefit explicitly or implicitly. Therefore, the public provision of education is based on the assumption that the participation in education of anyone confers benefits not only on the person but also on every other member of the community. It is then for each community to evaluate the amount of education for which it is ready to provide public financial support. However, education units are organized hierarchically, from basic up to higher education, and in turn each of these has its internal hierarchy. And then families do invest in the education of their children. A community may choose to cover only the costs of basic education for all, or it might consider that all education, regardless of its level, is free of charge for everybody who prove to have the capacities and the motivation for learning (a meritocratic perspective); or that it might provide only a subsidy for education, that is, an addition to parental expenditures for education.

When evaluating such options, one should consider both the internal effectiveness of educational organization and functioning, and its external efficiency in terms of its contribution to community development. Moreover, the funding of education as a "public good" from the public budget cannot ignore the investments made by families, private organizations and private persons. The problem is then one of reaching a Pareto optimality or efficiency, so that, thorough well being can be made without reducing any other person's well being. If so, then one should be looking into various specific contributions in terms of amounts and ways of complementing one another or in terms of choice functions and types of bargain.[11]

When considering the traditional meaning of the "public good" and higher education as a "public good," equal community payments by all would clearly favor those with high family incomes. The poor would then pay for the rich, through the taxation system, a situation that might be untenable for obvious moral, political, and financial reasons. One way out of this situation, when considering the hierarchical structure of education, is for the community to pay mostly for basic education, and for higher education to rely increasingly on private and family contributions. Such an option is strongly related to what C.L. Schultze calls "the public use of private interest,"[12] that is, the generation of a market for facilitating that use of private interests which would bring benefits to the community. Higher education should then be provided as a "public good" by relying not exclusively on public funds, but also (probably more) on private means, by introducing a system of "user charges." Thus private interests are put to use in the public domain, and, for the better operation of this option, the market would provide the most appropriate means.

In most of the European countries, higher education has, until recently, been considered as part of the public sector. Higher education was organized only through State-charted institutions while their services were delivered through a system of public administration based on an integrated command structure associated with a specific bureaucratic system. During the last two decades and mainly in the last ten years or so, new types of higher education institutions have emerged: corporate, private (for profit or not for profit), virtual, as well as mixtures of each of these types, thus generating a new academic landscape. A (quasi) market of higher education has started to operate both nationally and internationally, indeed globally. The provision of higher education as a public service has come to be challenged for its

inefficiencies and costs, while the new academic entrepreneurs, who have committed themselves to the delivery of a public service by relying on traditional market
mechanisms, have been confronted with important difficulties. V. Ostrom and E. Ostrom rightly pointed out
that "the *private* delivery of *public* services is a different
ball game from the *private* delivery of *private* goods and
services."[13] We are now faced in Europe with such challenges in higher education. A new understanding and
new policies have thus been required.

The launching of such a new approach to higher
education policy design and implementation may be
identified in Europe at the beginning of the 1980s, when
the Conservative government of Margaret Thatcher in
the United Kingdom initiated a strong criticism of the
public sector, including higher education, from the perspective of neo-liberal principles and ideology. The basic
idea was that since higher education as a public sector
demonstrated a high level of inefficiency, a lack of accountability and insufficient attention paid to consumers (customers), that is to students, it should be so ref-
ormed as to become subject to the rigors of market
mechanisms. While the "production functions" of the
sector (i.e., teaching, learning and research) were expected to remain much the same, their management and
evaluation were to be changed dramatically. A new paradigm began to be instituted which brought about
changes both in the language (borrowed mostly from
management and marketing theory), in policy making,
implementation and evaluation, and in the ways higher
education institutions should function as organizations.

The experiments initiated at the time were based on
such a market paradigm as to generate a higher educa-

tion market that could be steered by: *competition and efficiency, "value for money" and accountability, commodification of services which should be customer orientated, institutional entrepreneurship, and a new management focused on issues like strategic planning, quality assurance, responsiveness to demands, transfer of technology, and partnership with industry*. New managerial techniques, like *internal markets* and an *agency status for performance indicators* were put into use at both system and institutional levels. Universities have come to be seen as organizations that compete on the market and are accountable to stakeholders. Academic leaders are viewed as *managers*. Students are regarded as *customers or consumers*. Academics are *service providers* who are subject to consumer evaluation. Within the new competitive market paradigm, universities have been expected to develop appropriate *corporate strategies* at both functional and cultural levels. The emerging outcomes have been, among others, a whole set of "boundary objects," like those mentioned above, floating between the traditional codes of university life and the newly instituted market codes. A new higher education paradigm has started to take roots in the academic world of United Kingdom as well as in other European countries.

When surveying the dominant topics of discussion in the 1990s and later, one may easily observe the slow, but also the sure, emergence of those ones which are typical of the new higher education paradigm. As described above, a whole new set of "boundary objects" has emerged. These refer not only to policy and managerial issues. In addition to attempts to change the management of universities as organizations and to evaluate them in order to inform the consumers, many transformations have also been brought about in their internal "production functions," that is, in teaching and learning, in the organization of curricula and in the research activities undertaken. As for the latter, one may see how *scientific work has turned itself from the open, ethical community of scholarship, into a special type of trade*, where, for instance, *intellectual property* has to be submitted to new legal and corporate rules. The difference between the productivity and functions of academic research and the commercialization of its outputs has become blurred. University research has definitely started to be reconfigured as property (corporate and/or individual), and scholars are slowly being repositioned as *knowledge traders* and not simply as knowledge producers, transmitters, or reproducers. As Corynne McSherry put it,[14] "the university's traditional service mission, once construed as an obligation to provide tools for public decision-making, has been substantially redefined to mean the transfer of university research from academia to the market via patenting and licensing."

When looking at such changes, one might adopt one or two stances. The radical stance would emphasize the shift of paradigms, so that the university is slowly betraying its original functions in order to take up a new corporate role in the emerging higher education market. On the other hand, many of the changes would reveal a mixture of concepts, discourses, and practices originating both in the market and in the "public good" philosophies. Such a mixture would bring about the dominance of either one or both at the same time, so that the overall impression would be one of ambiguity, and indeed of uncertainty. Moreover, the discourses are shaped according to circumstances and to prospective external benefits. When "public good" concerns become dominant, the discourses focus on their advantages and are voiced strongly and widely. When the widening of the higher education market is explored, its corresponding discourses become more vociferous. The end result is not only one of ambiguity, but also of uncertainty. Which paradigm to follow in the further development of higher education is a question which has not yet received a final answer. We are in that age of modernity which demand for a new type of reflexivity. The parallel and mixed tracks of development are with us, they are occasionally clashing, a reality that can be easily observed by considering some other trends which refer to academic mobility and to certain changes in the academic space.

1.6. ACADEMIC MOBILITY AND CERTAIN OTHER TRANSFORMATIONS IN THE ACADEMIC SPACE

As explained above, GATS makes a distinction between various modes of service delivery while relating these to the modes of trade in services. The distinction is related to the ways a service is supplied to the beneficiary. On the other hand, different types of academic mobility are identified by considering how a student reaches a study program: either the student or the staff or the study program is moving around. When bringing together the old (academic mobility) and the new (GATS) terminology of higher education, one may notice that the modes of service delivery are closely related to the types of academic mobility, and both to the modes of trade in services. In order to further explore such relationships, let us firstly remember the basic notion of academic mobility as it was traditionally defined.

Student mobility refers to students moving in a given geographical and academic space. This space is circumscribed geographically by the borders between nation-states and continents and academically by more or less different historical and cultural traditions of higher education institutions. While in the early history of higher education student mobility was not influenced by any 19th and 20th centuries consecrated the university as a national symbol or as the key institution for the formation of national professionals, thus amending the universal or global dimension of higher education and of academic mobility. However, it was in the last quarter of the 20th century and onwards that the idea of the internationalization of higher education and of academic mobility started to take roots and to be extended to all universities. Subregional, regional, and even global programs of internationalization have been initiated and implemented, student mobility being part and parcel of such a program. One may thus identify three dimensions of the higher education space:

a) *national,* i.e., a system of higher education institutions belonging to a nation-state and providing the service of higher learning;
b) *regional,* i.e., an area which includes higher education institutions from several neighboring national systems of higher education. For instance, we are witnessing the emergence of the "European Higher Education Area" envisaged by the Bologna Declaration (19 June 1999) in Europe while also in Latin or North America certain developments of emerging regional areas of higher education are taking place;

c) *global*, i.e., a transnational (borderless) space of higher education which transcends the borders between nation-states belonging to different regions or continents.

Considering these dimensions, one may view student mobility as taking place between institutions from within a nation-state, and among institutions which belong to different national systems of higher education. Most importantly, the student is the mobile entity. In this enterprise, student mobility is also complemented by *staff* (teachers and researchers) *mobility*, in the sense that university teaching and/or research staff travel temporarily to another country to provide on a paying basis educational or research services in a higher education institution belonging to a specific country of destination.

In addition to student or staff mobility, one area which has recently been expanding very rapidly has been that of *study program mobility*. Instead of a student moving in space to reach a higher education institution, the study program of the institution moves in space to reach a higher number of students. The recent technological breakthroughs, particularly the new information and communication technologies (ICTs), have facilitated the mobility of study programs. Nowadays, one may rightly say that this type of mobility is experiencing the most rapid development, generating the so-called "borderless higher education" or transnational education. With the mobility of study programs, the traditional borders of higher education be they geographical or conceptual, have been suspended. The traditional space of higher education becomes increasingly borderless.[15] Such

developments are also associated with important transformations in the higher education landscape. Let us
mention some of these.

A new type of higher education institution has emerged—*the virtual university*—, operating not only nationally but transnationally, without any limits as to time
and space. Its study programs are delivered through
electronic media; it has almost no academic faculty of its
own, and only a small proportion of students aim for a
full degree. Some virtual universities are fully independent and accredited (such as the National Technology
University in the USA); others operate without much
content of their own, only as a website with various links
(as is happening with the California's Virtual University). Some others are private ventures, which act as
"corporate" or for profit universities, or are products of
partnerships or consortia of several institutions, including business enterprises.

Either through consortia partnerships or independ-
ently, many classical universities have embarked upon
teaching on-campus and off-campus students simultaneously. The ICT installments have helped them provide
courses to distant students, while also facilitating the
ongoing interaction with them in the study process.
Moreover, the conventional type of student may have
access to both the classical and the technologically
mediated type of teaching and learning, since the same
curricula are offered to both on- and off-campus students through the appropriate channels of communication. The basic question here is whether or not conventional universities will play the key role in the use of
ICTs and in the provision of e-learning or whether they
will lag behind. For the time being, many classical uni-

versities have opted for the development of e-learning facilities and also for keeping some of the "virtual institutions" under their auspices. Such developments are very much related to trading in higher education, and conventional universities have not hesitated to join the new type of institutions in order to sell their services. Here too one may observe that study program mobility is leading to the expansion of (virtual) student mobility, while also seizing market benefits. *The traditional academic paradigm is "polluted" by the generating codes and procedures specific to the market paradigm so that one does not quite know how to distinguish where one begins and the other ends.*

Such transformations in the landscape of higher education, which insist on the mobility of study programs, are well documented elsewhere in the literature.[16] In our search for "boundary objects," one may further insist on other transformations in higher education which are generated by factors such as: increase in student demand for higher education and diversification of student constituencies; new roles played by the traditional academic faculty and changes in the staffing of universities; dominance of new modes of knowledge production and transmission; and adoption of new managerial and organizational techniques. Any of the transformations associated with such factors illustrate one and the same thing: "boundary objects" are proliferating in higher education and in its associated discourses.

It is well known, for example, that the demand for higher education is growing all over the world, while the average age of students in classical universities is growing older and that of distance students, growing younger. However, such a uniform increase in demand for higher education is unevenly met by the national institutions in different countries. A World Bank report[17] mentions the "enrolment gap" that exists between the OECD countries and the developing countries and which has been expanding lately at a rapid pace. While in 1980, the tertiary enrolment rate in the United States was 55 percent and in the developing countries 5 percent, in 1995 the corresponding rates were 81 and 9 percent respectively. For the developing countries, the average rates hide huge discrepancies between countries and regions. As the World Bank report mentions, "the need to invest in expanding coverage at the tertiary level is nowhere more visible than in the large countries of Asia like China, India, and Pakistan with enrolment rates of 5, 6 and 3 percent respectively, or in those of Latin America like Brazil and Mexico, whose enrolment rate is less that 15 percent." *Such nationally unmet demands for higher education, combined with the facilities offered by the ICTs for off-campus or branch-campus higher education, have contributed to the recent expansion of transnational or borderless higher education and of trading in higher education services.* In addition, such transnational institutions provide services not only to traditional students ("learner-earner"), but also to the so-called "earner-learner" type of students, who are interested in their continuous professional development, and to the drop-outs who represent a considerable proportion in most higher education systems. It is then the growing student demand for higher education which generates certain academic developments and also provides incentives for a growing trade in higher education. No wonder then that the students are more and more regarded also as consumers or customers.

As for the academic staff, the most important challenge is represented by the recent trend of disaggregating the traditional teaching role in order to accommodate it with the increasingly specialized demands of high technology delivery and centralized curricula. The newly emerging modes of knowledge production and transmission are associated more often than not with "theory-light interdisciplines" which are included in the university curricula. These are process-oriented and focused on skills, putting the emphasis on "just-in-time" training and less so on the "just-in-case" learning which is so typical of classical universities. Research is less and less a key function of the academics, while their accountability for the quality of teaching is highly demanded. A clear trend of what S. Cunningham et al.[18] has called the "casualization" of the academic workforce has become obvious in higher education: shorter periods of annual employment (9–10 months), a higher number of part-timers or adjuncts, higher staff mobility coupled with the so-called "road scholars" who attempt to accumulate sufficient teaching hours in order to make a decent living. And these, again, provide incentives for extending, in this domain, the higher education market, while shrinking the traditional staffing and functioning of academic faculty.

Radical transformations have also taken place in the governance and management of higher education institutions, which have been brought in line with the philosophy and the techniques of the "new managerialism,"[19] as is appropriate to the market functioning of higher education. Without insisting on this development, it is important to explore those "boundary objects" which have appeared as a result of the interference of the new management actions, university curriculum design, and what M. Gibbons[20] calls "mode 2" of producing and communicating knowledge. Different from the classical "mode 1," which is focused on specialized and fragmented disciplines, the new "mode 2" approaches practical problems by developing transient and transdisciplinary teams, which draw on expertise from within and outside the university. In order to better cope with the requirements of the "mode 2" approaches, many universities have attempted to bring about appropriate changes in curriculum design and management structures which were also related to the best ways of seizing market opportunities opened up by the new client demands for training services. The end results have taken the forms of ambiguous, often contradictory "boundary objects": *managerial flexibility combined with a standardization of curriculum of a Fordist type in order to provide the expected "just in time" training; disaggregation of task roles in curriculum design and teaching combined with centrally developed "products," ready for an immediate use in training; corporate customization combined with a lack of customized curriculum for individual students; centralized leadership replacing the collegiate model of management; distortion of academic collegiate culture and its replacement by a fragmented staffing related to specialized and temporary training tasks without any research.* Indeed, many of these transformations are more obvious in the new higher education institutions and less so in the conventional ones. However, they have clearly started to also take root in the classical universities. As a matter of fact, over the last decade, the pace of change in this direction has been so rapid that the boundaries between the classical and the new (corporate, for-profit, virtual and the like) universities are no longer as clear as they used to be. The present societal and political environments force higher education institutions, new and conventional, to change in this direction in order for them to better respond to new demands, new markets and shifting consumer needs. The boundaries between different types of higher education institutions, new or classical, become more and more blurred, the "boundary objects" being the clear sign of such a process. Market forces and ICTs constitute the driving factors of the process of blending together the classical and the new, more market-oriented, universities.

1.7. CORRESPONDENCES BETWEEN GATS MODES OF SERVICES, TRADE AND INSTANCES OF ACADEMIC MOBILITY

In order to explore the blurring of boundaries between higher education institutions which are shaped out by either the traditional code or the market code, as well as their blending together, one should consider the correspondences which may be established between various types of academic mobility and the GATS modes of supplying higher education services which are also modes of trade in services. Table 1.1 illustrates the correspondences that result semantically from the meanings attached to each of their specific instances.

TABLE 1.1. *Correspondences between instances of academic mobility and GATS modes of services supply*

Mode 1: Cross-border supply: only the service itself crosses the border	*Mobility of study programs* mainly through the use of ICT in "virtual universities" (online teaching, e-learning)
Mode 2: Consumption abroad: A service consumer moves to another country to obtain the respective service	*Student mobility:* students moving in a given geographical and academic space (study abroad)
Mode 3: Commercial presence Commercial establishment of facilities abroad for providing a service	*Study programs mobility:* a higher education institution from the country A establishes a branch in the country B for providing a study program either independently or in partnership with a HEI from country B.
Mode 4: Presence of natural persons: a person travelling to another country on a temporary bas for providing a service.	*Staff mobility:* teachers, professors, researchers, instructors, etc. moving in the academic space from one HEI to another on a temporary basis for teaching or research purposes.

Some correspondences have also been outlined by other authors;[21] however, no direct connection with academic mobility has so far been identified. As Table 1.1 illustrates, there are obvious semantic and substantial correspondences between the GATS modes of supplying services and the types of academic mobility.

The oldest types of academic mobility have been those referring to student and staff mobility. They correspond straightforwardly with the GATS Mode 2 and 4 respectively. The newer type of academic mobility—that of study programs—corresponds to GATS Mode 1 (cross-border supply) and Mode 3 (commercial presence).

Both are associated with the development of transnational (borderless) education, which is strongly supported by ICTs and the emerging higher education markets.

These correspondences outline three important implications for our concerns here: (a) academic mobility evolved historically in a sort of "natural" way, responding to the internal needs of higher education, without necessarily being associated, at least in their earlier stages, with the requirements of the market codes; (b) however, since the 1980s, academic mobility and what in the GATS terminology is called "modes of services trade" are in close correspondence; (c) the semantic correspondences between the specific instances of GATS and academic mobility are so obviously straightforward that they do not pose any difficulties. Such implications deserve further analysis.

The semantic correspondences are based on the shared meanings of the terms used in the definitions of the types of academic mobility and of the GATS modes of supplying and trading a service. Apparently, only the terms are different, so that the same meanings could be conveyed or wrapped up by using different terms. It is, however, clear that the GATS terms are more appropriate for specifying a type of trade in services and not just one of supply of services. While issues specific to academic mobility could be easily translatable into those typical for any service trade, new meanings have also been attached. *The higher education market codes are at work here, substituting themselves for the traditional academic codes.* Which ones will become dominant is again a question for the future. At this stage, the two categories of codes co-exist and find themselves in close correspondence. "Boundary objects" provide appropriate bridges for more easily establishing the links between the two categories, while also generating ambiguities and uncertainties for those who are placed only on the other side of the fence.

We can take as an illustration such a "boundary object" as the internationalization of higher education with its old and newly associated meanings. For those associated with the academic traditional codes, internationalization is the response of academe to the demands of an increasingly interdependent world. Universities should provide opportunities to students for understanding different cultures, for improving their foreign language skills and for participating professionally in a world economy which is ever more globalized. For those associated with the market code, internationalization and trade may be separate as motives, but "they are in practice one and the same activity: any educational service provided by someone of a different nationality to the student is simultaneously a form of trade and a form of contact between two cultures."[22] Many other illustrations may be brought to the fore and they will convey the same messages as the ones associated with internationalization of higher education.

1.8. ACADEMIC MOBILITY AND TRADE
IN HIGHER EDUCATION

The above mentioned correspondences should be explored not only linguistically, in terms of language syntax or semantics. They have a substantial side, represented in quantitative terms, for approximating the amount of trade in higher education. We should indeed mention the *approximation* of trade in higher education, since, at this stage, it is difficult, as we will see, both to identify "trade in educational services" and to measure its amount.

In the attempts of the OECD to measure the size and to identify the trends in the international market in higher education, several difficulties have been encountered: statistics are not easily available and are not particularly reliable; data on educational services are often lumped together with those regarding other activities; the more recent developments in higher education are less transparent in terms of their activities abroad and almost no statistics are available. As these difficulties are mentioned in an OECD recent report, "it is therefore not easy, and sometimes impossible, to identify 'trade in education services' using standard statistics on services trade."[23] Despite these problems, the authors managed to provide a rough estimate of the size of trade in educational services in OECD countries. Considering the data available, they processed only that part of the data corresponding to GATS Mode 2—consumption abroad or, in the traditional academic terminology, to student mobility (students studying abroad).

Sometimes, these data are considered as estimating "the overall level of trade in educational services." For the period preceding the expansion of transnational (borderless) education, this indicator might be acceptable. However, since the middle of the 1990s, the use of ICTs and the rapid expansion of study programmes mobility have added new dimensions to trade in higher education. Mode 1: crossborder supply, and Mode 3, commercial presence, have become very active, and thus any estimation should consider their developments which have steadily become dominant.

In the attempts to measure the size of trade in higher education, one should consider: stages of higher education development, and the evolution of various types of academic mobility; and the availability of data and their reliability. The first two instances are highly correlated, in the sense that academic mobility evolves together with new developments in higher education. While up to the middle of the 1990s the mobility of study programmes was less expanded, it has, since then, started to involve a growing number of students and staff and new types of educational services (testing, consultancy and training, e-learning, etc.). It is indeed true that very few or almost no data are available for approximating the size of this mobility and of its corresponding trade, but this lack does not imply the use of the indicator on student and staff mobility as the only one for the estimation of the overall level of trade in higher education.

GATS and the study of trade in higher education find themselves confronted with an important problem: the traditional types of academic mobility or of modes of service supply are well in place and the information on their size and evolution is both available and reliable[24], but the new types of academic mobility, corresponding mostly to the market code, are less transparent. For instance, the OECD report estimates that "approximately 1.47 million foreign students in tertiary education were studying abroad in OECD countries in 1999," and that "the overall market in OECD of mode 2 trade in educational services is around $ US 30 billion in 1999, corresponding roughly to 3 percent of total trade in services in OECD countries."[25] The latter is again an underestimation, since not all educational services were included, particularly those associated with the mobility of study programs.

The situation in terms of correspondences between types of academic mobility and GATS modes of trade is such that those types of academic mobility and of modes that were generated by the traditional academic paradigm (student and staff mobility) are relatively transparent and well regulated, whereas those generated by the market code are less transparent and do not lend themselves to easy regulation by the traditional academic codes. We may thus be faced either with the need to reconstruct the academic space in order to include all its developments, traditional or new, or with a split between those developments that are regulated by the academic codes and those associated with the market codes. This challenge of options is the most important one facing higher education today at institutional, national and global level, being directly related to its roles and functions in any society.

1.9. A CONCLUSION

Trading in higher education is today one of the most important issues of academic concern. Its consequences are expected to become increasingly visible, not only in the ways conventional higher education institutions are to be organized and managed and in the newly emerging types of institutions, but also in the development of teaching, learning and research, in student flows, and in the staffing of universities, in the systemic distribution of academic power, both nationally with regard to the role of government in shaping public policies and in the funding of higher education, and internationally when considering the effects of borderless higher education and the dominance of the Anglo-American language and their types of institutions.

Anxieties, fears, ambiguities and uncertainties are associated with the advancement of trading. However, trading in higher education is not a new phenomenon. It is as old as student and staff mobility and the institutional charging of tuition fees for foreign students. What is new is the quantitative expansion of student mobility, facilitated, in addition, by the development of study program mobility. Also new is the institutionalization of GATS, which brings with it a new perspective on the old functioning of higher education at national and international level. But such novelties co-exist with well established academic traditions, and we are now faced with a clash between the two.

Higher education developments are indeed generated today by two paradigms. The academic paradigm was consecrated by the long history of the university and is widely shared by the existing conventional higher education institutions. More recently, a new market paradigm has been at work and, in combination with the impact of ICTs, has generated new developments in higher education. While each paradigm and its corresponding codes have specific discourses, practices and ideologies, a clash between them has emerged, being highly loaded with ambiguities and contingencies incorporated in "boundaries objects." When exploring the most frequent issues of concern in higher education today, one may easily see that they are related to "boundary objects" emerging out of the blending of the two paradigms. As a result, the academic space is currently clouded by many uncertainties. These are bound to influence the policies of institutional and systems development in an academic space which is becoming more and more globalized. For this reason, higher education finds itself confronted with a challenge that it has never before encountered: the requirement of its providing a coherent and consistent explanation to justify both its existence and functioning. Reflexive modernity is clearly at work here.

In doing so, it should further explore the implications of the two categories of generating and competing codes and paradigms and opt for those which best ensure its way of survival and optimal functioning. Take, for instance, academic quality assurance. In the last decade or so, a clear shift from the traditional collegiate model to the one borrowed from the managerial and marketing approaches has taken place in most of the higher education systems. However, the two models do not exclude each other, but rather coexist at the institutional and national level, while at the same time being loaded with tensions and uncertainties that originate in the regional (e.g., the emerging "European Higher Education Area") and in the global development of higher education. Academic mobility, credentials recognition and higher education trade demand new approaches to quality assurance, while the pressures of academic traditions are still to be considered. Thus the need for a quality framework that requires the establishment of an appropriate infrastructure of academic quality, which functions simultaneously at institutional, national and global level and reconciles old traditions with new approaches. Such a task seems to be today a top priority which can be approached only after reflecting on the links and implications of the two competing paradigms.

In a similar vein, one may consider student and staff mobility. From one perspective, outgoing and incoming students may show high imbalances for many countries in one direction or the other. Those with a high number of outgoing students and staff may talk of a "brain-drain" phenomenon with dramatic economic and social consequences. From a different perspective, those with a high number of incoming students and staff may regard it as a "brain-circulation" phenomenon with mutual benefits for all in an increasingly globalizing world. The two perspectives may hardly be considered as complementary from a traditional standpoint, but the globalizing waves of higher education and labor market blend them together and keep them going.

Many other similar examples may be brought to the fore in the same vein from almost all areas of higher education. It seems right to say that either the university is truly reinventing itself in order to cope with all the new challenges or it may slowly and surely be brought either to dissolution or to its replacement by new types of "learning organizations."

NOTES AND REFERENCES

1   Kit Carson, Bankrupt in a marketplace of ideology, *Higher Education Supplement,* 10 November 1999, p. 32. *See* S. Cunningham et al., *The Business of Borderless Education*, Department of Education, Training and Youth Affairs. Australia, 2000.

2 This may indeed be considered as a "transitional period" in higher education. However, the cognitive discourse, which is so to say epistemological by its very nature, follows closely or even anticipates and induces real (ontological) developments. The interplay of the two levels of reference may sometimes be hard to catch, this owing both to the ways the most prestigious and performing conventional universities will position themselves in the overall academic landscape and to the dynamics of development of the newly emerging higher education institutions. It is for this reason that the concept of "boundary object" is further introduced into the text, in the expectation that it will seize specific consequences of the interplay.

3 Ulrich Beck, *The Brave New Wold of Work*, Cambridge, Polity Press, 2000, p. 22.

4 Pierre Sauvé, *Trade, Education and the GATS: What's In, What's Out, What's All the Fuss About*, OECD-CERI, Paper prepared for the OECD/US Forum on Trade in Educational Services, 23–24 May 2002, Washington, D.C., USA.

5 Corynne McShery, *Who Owns Academic Work? Battling for Control of Intellectual Property*, Cambridge, MA, Harvard University Press, 2001, p. 7.

6 WTO, Council for Trade in Services, *Education Services. Background Note by the Secretariat,* S/C/W/49, 23 September 1998, p. 4.

7 Dr. Jane Knight, Trade in Higher Education Services: The Implications of GATS, *The Observatory of Borderless Higher Education*, March 2002, pp. 8–9; P. Altbach, Higher Education and the WTO: Globalization Run Amok, *International Higher Education,* Spring 2001; S. Sinclair, *How WTO's new "services" negotiations threaten democracy*, Canadian Centre for Policy Alternatives, September 2000; *Joint Declaration on Higher Education and the GATS,* issued by AUCC, ACE, CHEA and EUA, 28 September 2001; Donald Hirsch, *Report on "OECD/US Forum on Trade in Educational Services*," Washington, DC, USA, 23–24 May 2002. For recent data, see OECCD, *Science and Education Indicators 2008*. See also the 2008 OECD report, *Education at a Glance.*

8 *Op. cit.*, p. 1.

9 Vincent Ostrom and Elinor Ostrom, Public goods and public choices, in Michael D. McGinnis (ed.), *Polycentricity and Local Public Economies*, Ann Arbor, The University of Michigan Press, 1999, pp. 75–103.

10 P.A. Samuelson, The Pure Theory of Public Expenditure, *Rev. Econ. Stat.*, Nov. 1954, 3–6, pp. 387–89. *See* M.W. Pauly, Mixed Public and Private Financing of Education: Efficiency and Feasibility, *The American Economic Review*, 57, March 1967, pp. 120–30.

11 M.W. Pauly, *op. cit.*

12 C.L. Schultze, *The Public Use of Private Interest*, Washington, DC, The Brooking Institution, 1977.

13 V. Ostrom and E. Ostrom, *op. cit.*, p. 76.

14 C. McSherry, *op. cit.*, p. 2.

15 St. Cunningham et al., *op. cit.*; CVCP, *The Business of Borderless Education: UK Perspective*, 2002. CEURC, *Transnational Education Report* (2001), Confederation of European Union Rectors.

16 A recent synthetic view on the matter is presented in the special issue of the UNESCO–CEPES review *Higher Education in Europe:* Virtual versus Classical Universities: "Conflict or Collaboration?" 26/4, 2001.

17 World Bank, *Constructing Knowledge Societies: New Challenges for Tertiary Education,* 2002, pp. 29–30.

18 S. Cunningham et al., *op. cit.*, p. 118 passim.

19 D. Warner, D. Palfreyman (eds.), *Higher Education Management. The Key Elements*, Buckingham, SRHE & O.U.P. Press, 1996.

20 M. Gibbons, *Higher Education Relevance in the 21st Century*, The World Bank Education, 1998; M. Gibbons, C. Limoges, H. Nowotny, S. Schwartzman, P. Scott, M. Trow, *The New Production of Knowledge: Science and Research in Contemporary Societies*, London, Sage, 1994.

21 J. Knight, *op. cit.*; K. Larsen, J.P. Martin, R. Morris, *Trade in Educational Services: Trends and Emerging Issues*, CERI, OECD, Working Paper, 2002.

22 D. Hirsch (Rapporteur), *OECD/US Forum on Trade in Educational Services*, Washington, DC, USA, 23–24 May 2002, p. 4.

23 Larsen et al., *op. cit.*, p. 3.

24 The flows of foreign student enrollment in the countries of the UN Europe Region were studied periodically by different UNESCO–CEPES teams: *Higher Education and Economic Development in Europe,* vol. II, CEPES, Bucharest, 1983; *Enseignement Supérieur en Europe*, CEPES, vol. XI, No. 1, 1986; *Higher Education in Europe*, CEPES, vol. XIII, No. 3, 1988; *Statistics on Higher Education. 1980–1985: A Study of Data on Higher Education and Research from the Countries of the Europe Region*, CEPES, 1989.

25 Larsen et al., *op. cit.*, p. 10.

CHAPTER 2
Demography and Higher Education: Risks and Prospective Approaches

A new factor has been consistently brought to the fore within the framework of higher education policy analysis and design. This factor refers to demographic prospects as they include issues related to demography *per se*, as well as to others of a wider reference, such as migration flows and changes in lifestyles and lifecycles of individuals in this time of high modernity.

There are many reasons for bringing in higher education policy framework issues related to demographic prospects. Some are induced by the implications of the recent transition of most of the European systems of higher education from elite-oriented to mass or universal systems, in Martin Trow's terminology.[1] From such a perspective, when a country's population declines and the higher education system becomes mass-oriented, its institutions should not only consider their policies related to traditional issues such as teaching and learning resources, curriculum design or funding and institutional governance, but also to the demographic sustainability of the mass system. Other reasons are exogenous to the higher education systems and are generated either by changes in qualifications and the labor market, associated as they are with a widely emerging new economy, or by those demographic projections, which are so common to economists in their analysis of a labor market's prospects, as well as by changes in life-cycles and lifestyles, as identified by psychologists or sociologists in their analysis of the so called post-materialist society.[2] For instance, during the period of the recent demographic transition, most European countries have been confronted with growing population declines, increased migration flows and an ageing population. Changes in lifecycles and lifestyles have also made education increasingly important in the lives of all individuals, thus increasing the demand for higher levels of education.

It appears that, considering the impact of demographic prospects on higher education policy, two assumptions hold a key position. On the one hand, one may take the view that the expansion of student flows questions the sustainability of a mass higher education system when confronted with a demographic decline in the country of concern. On the other hand, it is possible to demonstrate, as some may do, that the elite higher education systems would have turned into mass systems as a result of the pressure put on them by the demographic and individual demand side of the system, regardless of actual or prospective demographic flows. In what follows, such assumptions are further explored; mainly by relying on those facts which demonstrate that higher education expansion has occurred both under demographic growth and decline, and that the sustainability of expansion may not necessarily depend on demography alone.

When approaching these issues, it may prove beneficial to explore various alternative options and dilemmas, thus arriving at a better understanding of the demographic impact on higher education policies, particularly at institutional level. However, it cannot be denied that demographic prospects have so far received "only minimal or short-sighted attention among decision makers at the political as well as the institutional level."[3] This has happened, as many others argued, despite the growing mismatch between the excess supply of higher education and the shrinking demand due to population decline in many European countries. How such developments are brought into the analytical framework and what policy implications they may have therefore demand further reflection. Particularly when considering the social, economic, cultural, political and indeed the academic risks generated in most of the European countries by the current demographic decline.

In what follows, the analysis will be initiated by taking a closer look at some demographic trends and developments in Europe. This will help to further the reflection on certain options and dilemmas regarding the demographic impact on higher education policy. Finally some implications for institutional policies will be identified.

2.1. THE DEMOGRAPHIC "TYRANNY OF NUMBERS" AND SOME COMPLEMENTARITIES

The sheer scale of today's higher education determines a great deal of how it operates, how it is related to economy and labor market, and how people's lives are affected. But most of all the present size of higher education is inevitably related to demographic prospects since they reveal how past growth is sustainable in the shorter or longer run. To begin with, let us consider the global level. Table 2.1 summarizes both the total number of students in the world and the increase in numbers since 1980. They all show what by now is well known, that the numbers of students have constantly increased, to the point where, at the turn of the new millennium, no less than one in five of the globe's inhabitants were registered as a student in all levels of formal education. Over the last 25 years the highest increase in numbers occurred in higher education, which almost doubled, while the proportion of primary and secondary school students has constantly decreased.

There are now, in Europe alone, enrolment rates in higher education that have grown from 10–15 percent to over 40 percent, and in many countries to well over 60 percent of the entire eligible age group. In the UN Europe Region (Europe, North America and Israel), the proportion of tertiary students in the total number of students has increased from 15.7 percent to more than 23 percent.

The reason for such an increase is twofold. On the one hand, for most European governments, universities are at the hub of the knowledge economy, acting as powerful drivers of technological and other changes critical to national economic and social development. From this point of view, participation levels in higher education have been constantly increased and a growing number of routes to higher education have been offered. On the other hand, the individual demand for higher education degrees has also constantly increased.

TABLE 2.1. *World population and students: 1980–2005*

Year	1980	1991	1999	2005
Total population	4,447,081,447	5,461,689,400	5,978,702,000	6,477,001,177
Total students	856,971,000	995,948,000	1,169,502,963	1,339,110,773
% Students of total population	19.27%	18.24%	19.56%	20.67%
Primary and secondary students	805,935,000	925,598,000	1,086,253,401	1,201,180,045
% Primary and secondary students of total students	94.04%	92.94%	92.88%	89.70%
Tertiary students	51,037,000	70,350,000	97,664,562	137,930,727
% Tertiary students of total of students	5.96%	7.06%	8.35%	10.30%

Sources: UNESCO Institute of Statistics (UIS) databases; UNFPA, 1997, 2005; FAO Population Service, 1997.

TABLE 2.2. *Population and students in Europe:*
1980–2005

Year	1980	1991	1999	2005
Total population	1,001,350,000	1,014,146,400	1,032,702,000	1,128,652,995
Total students	178,926,760	205,967,110	219,867,637	225,039,250
% Students of total population	17.87%	20.31%	21.29%	19.94%
Primary and secondary students	150,820,078	170,526,722	177,666,998	172,203,321
% Primary and secondary students of total students	84.29%	82.79%	80.81%	76.52%
Tertiary students	28,106,682	35,440,388	42,200,639	52,835,929
% Tertiary students of total of students	15.71%	17.21%	19.19%	23.48%

Sources: UIS data bases; UNFPA, 1997, 2005; FAO Population Service, 1997.

The highlight of such reasons is obviously influenced by demography, and the analysis of the demographic impact on higher education is mostly, if not entirely, based on numbers. One regards how demographic growth or decline is related to student flows, and highlights either an increase or decrease in the higher education recruiting pool. The argument goes further by showing how the demographic prospects that emerge in a specific country would spill over into other areas of social and economic development, since higher education trains the best qualified labor force in any country and promotes key cultural and social values. Numbers regarding changes in areas of employment and their relation to labor market demands, work productivity and economic development rates are then referred to the flow of educational qualifications for evaluating the (mis)match between labor demand and supply. An endless array of numbers are invoked and compared, and so demography comes in with its own prospects, holding a key position in the demonstration. It might be said that a "tyranny of numbers" is at work. And this also raises various concerns related to the risks for social development or uncertainties embedded in demographic prospects and with regard to their impact on *inter alia* higher education. However, the question is: *should we consider only the "numbers" and demographic prospects alone or should we combine them with other factors at work in order to better asses their joint impact on higher education?*

Demography has arrived late, and in fact only very recently entered analytical frameworks focusing on higher education. This entry coincided with the passing of higher education from an elite-oriented system to a mass and in some countries universal system, as well as with the arrival of what economists use to call "the new economy." For an elite-oriented system, demography was of a little concern. Whatever the size of the population in a country, the existing higher education institutions, small and elite as they were, had a sufficient number of candidates without having to worry about the demographic prospects. Since the number of higher education institutions has grown at a rapid pace and individual demand for higher qualifications awarded by colleges and universities came from a much larger pool of individuals, higher education systems have been expanding dramatically. Let us look more closely at this expansion.

2.2. NUMBERS AND FLOWS
OF STUDENTS

Over most of the twentieth century higher education expanded steadily and slowly together with secondary schooling. Before the Second World War there were no more, probably less, than 2 percent of young people enrolled in degree programs in almost all European countries. After 1960 the proportions started to grow. Within a generation, since the 1980s and 1990s, university attendance has become a normal pattern for most young people. Alison Wolf has shown how, in a few decades, following developments in the USA, many other systems of higher education followed the same route (Figure 2.1.).

By the end of the twentieth century higher education turned into a universal system in the USA, and into mass systems in France, Germany, Italy or the UK. During the period 1995–2005 participation in tertiary

FIGURE 2.1. *Participation rates in higher education: percentage of age cohort entering higher education USA*

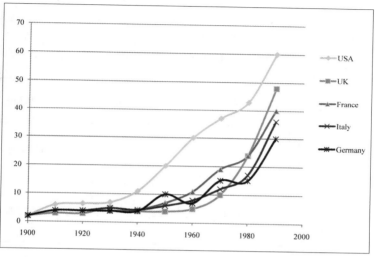

Source: Alison Wolf (2002),[4] p. 173.

education grew in absolute terms on average by 50%, while entry rates increased in 2004 by 20% compared to 2000. The USA has now a gross enrolment ratio in higher education of over 80%, Poland and Sweden are close to 60%, Canada has arrived at 59%, while on average countries of the EU have reached 52%.

The data are clear: today almost all higher education systems in Europe are either mass or universal higher education systems. A "graduate society" is emerging in Europe, with an average of about a half of the age group following and eventually graduating academic routes. European countries also aim to mirror to the USA where more than two thirds of the age cohort enters tertiary education.

TABLE 2.3. *Student population in the UN Europe Region:*
numbers and their subsequent graphic illustration

Year	1980	1991	1999	2005
Total population	1,001,350,000	1,014,146,400	1,032,702,000	1,128,652,995
Total students	178,926,760	205,967,110	219,867,637	225,039,250
% Students of total population	17.87%	20.31%	21.29%	19.94%
Primary and secondary students	150,820,078	170,526,722	177,666,998	172,203,321
% Primary and secondary students of total students	84.29%	82.79%	80.81%	76.52%
Tertiary students	28,106,682	35,440,388	42,200,639	52,835,929
% Tertiary students of total of students	15.71%	17.21%	19.19%	23.48%

Sources: UIS databases; UNFPA, 1997, 2005.

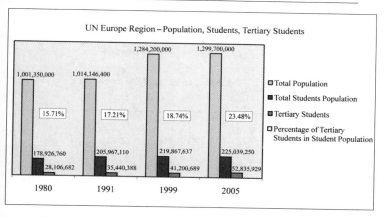

UN Europe Region – Population, Students, Tertiary Students

- Total Population
- Total Students Population
- Tertiary Students
- Percentage of Tertiary Students in Student Population

	1980	1991	1999	2005
Total Population	1,001,350,000	1,014,146,400	1,284,200,000	1,299,700,000
Total Students Population	178,926,760	205,967,110	219,867,637	225,039,250
Tertiary Students	28,106,682	35,440,388	41,200,689	52,835,929
Percentage of Tertiary Students in Student Population	15.71%	17.21%	18.74%	23.48%

Such an expansion of higher education is also reflected in the increase in the number of years a child can expect to spend in some form of formal education Table 2.4).

During the period from 1995 to 2005, education expectancy increased by around 12%, so that by 2005 a 5-year-old person could expect to spend 2 more years in education than a decade earlier. Females could expect to spend, on average, a longer period of time in formal education than males, though in countries such as Germany or Turkey males spend longer time than females. The increase in education expectancy is due to higher participation in pre-school education, to retaining a higher percentage of students until the end of their teenage years, and also to an increase in participation at the tertiary level. In most European countries an 18-year-old may expect on average to receive today 3 years of tertiary education, of which 2.3 years will be full-time.

When higher education becomes mass or universal, demographic prospects should be explored in order to demonstrate the sustainability in the shorter or longer run. However, in doing so, a distinction between the

TABLE 2.4. *Education expectancy in*
selected countries

No. of years of education expectancy	Education expectancy by country
21	
20	UK (20.7) Sweden (20.3)
19	
18	
17	Germany (17.4) Spain (17.2) Poland (17.0) Italy (17.0)
16	USA (16.9)
15	Russian Federation (15.0)
14	
13	
12	Turkey (12.6)

massification of higher education and the sustainability of existing student flows should be made. Higher education massification refers to the percentage of the relevant age cohort that enrolls in higher education. This percentage may grow, while the absolute numbers of student flows may fall. The demographic prospects do not affect the sustainability of a mass or universal system of higher education, but the absolute numbers of student flows. This is illustrated by numbers in Table 2.5.

Taking the year 2005 as reference and the demographic prospects for the year 2015, we see that individual countries may expect changes in the estimated percentage of tertiary students due to changes in the size of the population. Poland, Romania and the Russian Federation face reductions of around 30% or more in the population corresponding to upper secondary education over the next ten year period. They may thus be con-

TABLE 2.5. *Expected years in tertiary education and changes in tertiary enrolment (1995 = 100), 2004*

| | Expected no. of years in tertiary education | | | Changes in enrolment (1995 = 100) | |
| | *Male and Female* | *Female* | *Total tertiary education* | *Attributable to* | |
				Change in population	Change in enrolment rates
Estonia	3.3	4.1	269	—	—
Germany	2.	2.3	108	84	12
Italy	2.9	3.3	116	—	—
Poland	3.3	3.9	269	—	—
Romania	2.5	2.7	173	91	197
Russian Fed.	3.	3.8	190	97	193
Spain	3.0	3.4	120	92	128
Sweden	3.0	3.4	152	95	161
Turkey	1.5	1.3	168	114	150
UK	2.8	3.2	124	99	126
USA	4.1	4.8	—	—	—

Source: UIS, 2006; UN Statistics Division; OECD, 2006.

fronted with a decrease in the number of candidates to tertiary education. The number of graduates of tertiary education will decrease sharply in Spain (34%) over the next ten years and the same may happen in Italy, Poland, Romania and the Russian Federation. However, this trend may be reversed by increasing the participation rate in higher education, including increases in the number of graduates of upper secondary education and in lifelong education programs. Increases in the number of tertiary graduates and also in participation rates may occur in Sweden, the UK, the USA or Germany.

TABLE 2.6. *Demographic trends—2005/2015—and*
prospective tertiary education enrolments (OECD data):
numbers and subsequent graphic illustration

	Change in the size of the population 2005/2015 (2005 = 100)		Estimated percentage change in the number of new tertiary students between 2005 and 2015
	15–19 age group	20–29 age group	
Germany	86	104	4
Italy	96	85	−15
Poland	69	82	−18
Romania	71	93	−16
Russian Fed.	55	85	−15
Spain	91	66	−34
Sweden	84	117	17
Turkey	108	100	0
UK	92	113	13
USA	100	113	13

Countries are ranked in descending order of the size of the 15-to-19 year old pop-
ulation (2005 = 100).
Trends in the number of new tertiary graduates follow projections of the popula-
tion aged 20-to-29 and assume current graduation rates.
Source: OECD (2006),[5] UNESCO Institute of Statistics (UIS) (2005).

The conclusion seems to be obvious: when a country is confronted with a demographic decline the number of student flows is decreasing. However, the participation rate in higher education may grow in relative terms with reference to the specific age cohort and even to a wider pool of candidates to higher education coming from the older population.

2.3. SOME COMPLEMENTARITIES

Conventional demography has encountered certain difficulties in understanding and explaining demographic behavior and change. Such difficulties originate in the impossible task of a "perfect" measurement and in the lack of exploration of the meanings attached to behaviors being measured. The potential increases in relative, and not necessarily absolute, terms of student flows described above are based on several assumptions and on their corresponding evidence. Some of these assumptions, together with their implications, are explored below, in order to highlight some complementarities between demographic numbers/rates and some specific changes of a qualitative type in society and in the social demand for higher education.

i) *Growing individual demand for higher education.*
   It is clear that the main factor driving expansion in tertiary enrolments is the growing individual demand for higher education. This may be explained in terms of:
- individual rational choices, considering labor market incentives for having a higher education degree;
- recent public policies promoted by most national governments for increasing higher education participation rates;

- social and political pressure for increasing the participation in higher education of various minorities
  groups (ethnic groups, persons with disabilities,
  women, etc.);
- the pressures of the new economy demands for higher qualifications.

These four factors have had the same converging effect:
a growing number of teenagers and adults are increasingly rejecting or are not content with only specialized
vocational courses in secondary schools. High school
teenagers favor more academically oriented courses
that help them opt for tertiary education. Upper secondary and higher education then run convergent: the
growing increase in the former is followed by a growing
number of students in the latter. A person with a general education received in the upper secondary school
has almost no vocational qualification, but is well qualified for entering into higher education, which assures
good post-graduation prospects for joining those graduates who have a better position in the society and are
better paid. Adults who see an increase in graduate
numbers also feel the need to enrol in higher education.
The growing individual demand for higher education is
thus the end product of the individual rational choices
that are shaped by the new dominating meanings
attached to qualifications in today's world. A. Wolf
seems to be right when answering the question that
regards the global expansion of higher education in the
following way: "Not (though governments hold the
purse strings) from any conscious international agreement or resolution. And not because of any simple
growth in the economy's 'need' for graduates either:
there was no dramatic change in late twentieth century

occupations that can parallel the surge in student number. Rather, enrolments take off because and when things reach a point of no return: at a certain level of participation, potential students are destined—or doomed—to join in."[6]

The implication of this argument would take the form of the "snowball effect": when a level of participation in higher education reaches a critical point, individual demand will grow, and higher education student flows are bound to increase. There are then good chances that the present mass systems of higher education in Europe will become and remain universal systems, regardless of demographic decline or growth. The demographic impact refers to the sustainability of existing student flows in absolute terms and not in relative terms. Moreover demographic decline may not impact only on the demand side of the system, but mostly on the supply of higher education. A reverse tide seems to be in the offing. While previously the increasing demand for higher education led to an increase in supply, the future may bring with it a sharp shrinking and stratification in the supply of higher education. Some higher education institutions might be forced to merge with others or close, while others, already better positioned, would consolidate their positioning in the hierarchy.

ii) *Changes in age distribution of the population and in individual lifecycles/lifestyles* also influence higher education student flows, just as they bear on other social processes. The age structure of the population in Europe has changed as a consequence of decreasing fertility and mortality. Life expectancy has been constantly increasing and, combined with low fertility rates, has led to a shift in the relative weight of the

population from younger to older groups. Most European societies are confronted with an ageing population, a feminization of ageing (especially true of
the oldest old) and with a diminishing number of
children and young people.

Population ageing began in Europe at the end of the
nineteenth century, together with the first demographic
transition, but recent trends and projections show that
the ageing process is accelerating. As a UN demographic analysis demonstrated,[7] the number of children in
Europe dropped below that of older persons for the
first time in 1998. Since then, population ageing has
constantly increased. While currently over a fifth of
Europe's population is aged 60 years or over, by 2050
the proportion of people over 60 is expected to be double
that of children (up to 15), reaching the level of almost
a third of the population. The population of older persons is also ageing, the number of the persons aged 80+,
majority women, is growing at a pace of 3.9 percent per
year. This trend bears directly on inter-generational and
intra-generational equity and solidarity, and also has
important economic, social and educational consequences. Population ageing does imply a significant increase
in public spending, an increased dependency ratio and
the risk of depopulation. Nevertheless ageing should be
also regarded as a human success story. It is not merely
a matter of accumulating years. It should also be regarded as a process of adding life to years and not only
years to life.

While much attention has so far been paid to the economic and social consequences of population ageing in
Europe, particularly those of labor market demands and
the operation of welfare systems, educational implica-

tions have been barely mentioned. This may be due to the typical demographic approach, which is mostly quantitatively oriented. However, when considering more qualitative information, demographic changes overtime and their educational impact may be regarded from a more elaborated perspective. Consider, for instance, specific shifts in value orientations. The sociologist Ronald Inglehart[8] demonstrated that in most developed countries a shift from materialist to post-materialist values has been taking place since the end of the twentieth century as a result of a process of inter-generational value change. Such a shift is related to changes in both lifestyles and lifecycles. The implication is that population replacement is not the only factor at work. It is strongly complemented by inter-generational value changes. Providing that economic security is assured, as in most European countries, lifecycles cease to follow the traditional linear path, and lifestyles are less connected with social classes and traditional values. Instead of following the linear path of moving from the playground to school and then to work, activities related to education, work and leisure alternate all the way through the age of maturity.

Returning to formal education in the later cycles of life, embedding learning into work on a continuous basis, emphasizing the pragmatic aspects of learning and others of the same sort point to two trends: (i) though education is and remains predominantly related to earlier stages of life, a growing number of individuals embark on education programs in later stages of their life; (ii) boundaries between activities like education, work and leisure are being increasingly blurred, thus allowing for multiple combinations. The implication is that enrolments in education should be explored not only with regard to specific and fixed ages or lifecycles. In their later stages of life individuals return to education for enhancing their knowledge and skills. They are more prone to do so as a consequence of the rapid pace of change in technology, economy or culture, but also as a way of achieving objectives of self-realization, so important in a growingly individualized society.[9] Individual demand for higher education, dominant as this may be for young people aged 18 to 24 years, is growing also among older people. The pool of candidates to higher education degrees is no longer limited to younger persons. The demographic reserve among older groups seems to be very large indeed.

Two trends are then to be identified. Firstly, the young population decline leads to a diminishing pool of candidates to higher education. Secondly, changes in lifestyles and lifecycles would lead to an increase in life-long learning and in higher education demand of older individuals.

iii) *Changes in the structuring of higher education systems* are also to be considered with regard to the future shaping of higher education student flows. As higher education has exploded in size, it has also changed structurally. It has become increasingly differentiated and hierarchical, both within and between countries, faced more or less with financial shortages. Looking ahead, many expect higher education to be confronted with a further institutional stratification, a growing competition between institutions both within and between countries in a global market, and an increasing pressure and controversy over costs and financial resources.

Pressures on institutions are greater today because of the functioning of mass higher education and of the global higher education market. In such circumstances, could it be the case that, in what Frank and Cook[10] used to call a "winner-take-all" society spawned by globalization, some higher education institutions have positioned themselves at the top and there is no way to change this? Or do inter-institutional arrangements and positioning change over time? In answering such questions let us refer to the way employers deal with the business of hiring new graduates. Faced with an increasing number of graduates, when hiring a young graduate, a personnel officer has to choose from a long list of candidates. Choosing the most qualified candidate with the best prospects of development implies the use of specific tests and information to increase the probability of identifying the best. Among the relevant information, a key factor is the institutional prestige of some, very few, universities. This may explain the explosion of ranking or league tables which are global, regional or national, and which often help company human resources departments to inform their decision on hiring new recruits, and students-to-be to select their study programs and institutions. The more prestigious an institution is, the better are its graduates' chances for employment and its pool of candidates to increase. Higher education institutions are thus, one way or the other, continuously stratified hierarchically. This development is also strengthened by the social stratification of students. There is substantial evidence that demonstrates that the richer the family the more likely it is that its offspring would go to a highly selective institution (Table 2.7). The institutional prestige of a university and the increasing entry pressure of candidates go hand in hand. The probability of a prestigious university being faced with a shortage of entry candidates is so low that it does not deserve any serious concern. Demographic decline may thus only affect less prestigious higher education institutions. While there are many private colleges in the U.S. that are considerable less prestigious than state funded universities like Michigan, the University of California, Berkeley and Virginia, the overall pattern of more affluent families' children attending prestigious private colleges remains true. In addition, a sharp hierarchy of prestige also exists within the public sector, with leading state-funded universities, often identified as the "public Ivies" in reference to Harvard, Princeton, and other elite universities, enrolling disproportionately more affluent students than the less prestigious state institutions.

TABLE 2.7. *Proportions of college students from different family income groups attending public/private colleges of all types in the USA (1997)*[11]

	Private colleges	State funded (public) colleges
Low income families (<$ 20,000)	18.9%	81.1%
Upper income families (upper $ 100,000–$ 200,000)	35.3%	64.7%
Richest families (> $ 200,000)	51.0%	49.0%

A sort of self-reinforcing mechanism is at work: students want to enter the best university they can and universities want to be and/or remain at the top by recruiting both top students and staff. However, this may not be taken for granted. Since the market positioning of a higher education institution is very much dependent on its reputation to attract best talents, each higher education institution tends to maintain and rely on that pool of candidates which proves to be most competitive.

Generating a hierarchical differentiation of higher education institutions is contrary to an egalitarian system in which all institutions have the same status. Comparisons between higher education systems show that some, like the American system, are more stratified, while others, like those of Central Europe, are more homogeneous. The question here is also one that regards inequalities of provision and prestige. Much of the evidence today suggests that accepting a high homogeneity coincides with low incentives for creativity, innovation and efficiency, while allowing for the stratification which emerges from competition means rejecting any uniformity in institutional performances. From a strict national perspective the option for a more uniform system may prove much more attractive politically. But in a global context it may prove less beneficial, mainly when considering that it may be hard to opt out of global pressures for differentiation when students, researchers and professors are offered a wider range of options for better condition of research work and salaries. Student and staff recruitment has increasingly ceased to be national, let alone local. It takes place across the borders. Universities chase the best researchers and students across borders. The process is facilitated by the available communication technologies and also by the new *lingua franca*—English—which is widely spoken across the academic and research world. A higher education system that chooses to be closed nationally and is inadequate when confronted with global academic developments may end up having less students and competitive staff and isolating itself from the world around it, regardless of national demographic prospects. This may be well illustrated by flows of migration and mobility.

iv) *Migration and mobility*

Migration and population decline in the Europe Region, coupled with issues of cultural diversity, are a source of major concerns today. Sometimes they are also put in a sort of paradoxical terms. For instance, one perspective is that migration may lead to an increase of cultural diversity which may reach an unmanageable level of inter-cultural conflict. From another perspective, migration is the solution to demographic shortages for the further expansion of the developed world as well as to the need for poverty alleviation in those less developed countries that are faced with a demographic surplus. For some, immigration is threatening when considering the potential floods of people to developed countries bent upon exploiting their welfare systems and educational facilities.

Migration and demographic challenges bring about new policy and political dilemmas that refer to such crucial issues as regional, national, social and personal security, diversity and identity. These three issues are strongly inter-related as they generate anxieties and uncertainties which run deeply at personal level and widely at national and community level.

TABLE 2.8. *International migration flows*

	International migrants millions	World population billions	Share of inter-national migrants in world population
1975	85	4.1	2.1%
1985	105	4.8	2.2%
1995	164	5.7	2.9%
2000	175	6.0	2.9%
2004	185	6.3	2.9%

Source: UN population databases.

The data in Table 2.8 show that international migration is growing on a global scale. The EU and the USA today have almost the same immigrant population, though Europe has only recently become a destination for a growing number of international migrants. In 2001 Europe had a share of 3.0‰, while the USA had 3.1‰ of international migrants in world population. 31% of the US population growth in the 1990s was due to international migration and this share is growing. Almost the same is true for Europe. A shortage of skills and labor, due to ageing and decreasing population in the developed European countries, is thus associated with an increase in international migration. Canada, Australia, New Zealand and the USA see immigration as a permanent process and institute special incentives to increase the immigration of students and highly-skilled workforce (e.g., green card lotteries, special scholarship schemes, research grants, etc.). The 2000 Lisbon strategy of the EU stresses the importance of labor migration as a means of addressing labor gaps, while the 1999 Bologna Declaration emphasized the need to increase higher education and research attractiveness of Europe and extend student mobility and "brain circulation."

Replacement or compensatory migration is more and more seen as that increase of immigration which is needed to maintain certain parameters of population. The implications of such policies are important for most developed European countries. Population decline is compensated, at least partially, by an increase in international migration. National student population declines in some countries are associated with an increasing number of immigrants (temporary or permanent), thus the emerging phenomenon of replacement migration. Compensatory migration diminishes demographic declines in developed countries and opens up new competitive forces in developing countries (brain drain, brain waste, brain circulation) that affect student flows and participation rates in higher education.

* * *

Now let us review the previous data. It seems obvious that the impact of demographic prospects on higher education is far from uniform in all countries of the Europe Region. However, certain general trends may be identified:

a) most European countries are confronted with a demographic decline and with an ageing population that may lead to a diminishing number of young candidates to higher education;
b) the individual demand for higher education stands a good chance of growing with regard to both younger and older persons;

c) international migration and academic mobility may also grow, affecting differentially national systems and institutions of higher education; some would be more attractive for immigrants and mobile students/staff, while others would rather be suppliers of migrants and academically mobile students and researchers; compensatory and replacement migration and brain circulation are growing and bear directly on national and institutional higher education policies.

Such trends, general as they are, underline the importance of demographic factors in the analysis of higher education. However, the question that should be raised is: should demography be considered alone or in a combination of contextualized factors?

2.4. CONSEQUENCES OF
AN APPROACH

Politics aside, one may reflect on the impact of demographic prospects on higher education by adopting:

- either *a factor-oriented approach*, which takes factors one by one as well as their interactions in order to explore their individual and aggregated impact on higher education;
- or *a context-oriented approach*, which focuses on how various contexts are shaped by different factors at work, and how they include higher education in a specific way.

Each of the two approaches has merit. The question is whether such approaches, in which demography is but one factor to be considered, aim to demonstrate the need of sustaining either the further expansion of student flows, or the *status quo* of the current expansion, or indeed the holding back of student flows. The most dramatic of these variants is the third one, and this is based on the assumption that the size of a population in general and particularly that of those aged 18+ is getting so small that the demand for higher education is necessarily declining with dramatic consequences for higher education and economic sustainability of a nation-state. Such a perspective is also based on two restrictive assumptions:

a) the spatial closing of each nation-state, so that its borders do not allow various individuals from moving in or out or does so only in limited and controlled ways;
b) the national embeddedness of higher education systems, so that each higher education institution belongs to and is embedded in a national system, relying entirely and exclusively on national, including demographic, resources.

In order to better explore the implications of such assumptions, it seems important to refer to the consequences of globalization. From this perspective, the following global developments are important:

- *global population shifts*, which are triggered by the growing inequalities and differences between various national states and regions, and generate an increasing migration of population; this includes also student mobility across borders;

- *migration of higher education study programs*, which is mostly, but not only, due to the use of information and communication technologies; program mobility is increasingly substitute for student mobility: instead of a student moving where a program is located the program moves where the student is located;
- *study program sharing, or joint study programs*, which allows students to take advantage of two or more academic worlds, including those that belong to and are confronted with over- and under-populations.

2.5. CONTEXTUALIZING DEMOGRAPHIC PROSPECTS

When considering such global developments, it is hard to accept the view that demography by itself and separated out from the social, cultural, economic and political contexts would provide a good platform for explaining current developments in higher education. For instance, let us consider the recent expansion of higher education in most European countries as well as in other parts of the world. While student flows have been growing to the level of turning most of the European higher education systems into mass or universal systems of higher education, national population has been stagnant or has even declined. Higher education expansion has not been generated by any demographic shifts, but by a growing individual and economic demand for higher education qualifications. As participation rates in higher education have been constantly growing many folds, the question is whether this trend is sustainable in the medium and even short term, given fertility rates, national age pyramids and other demographic measures. Two answers may come to the fore immediately. One is that institutional policies of recruiting students and designing study programs must be changed, and the second, complementary to the former, is that lifelong learning programs must be opened up and expanded in order to address new types of older students, while also attracting foreign students from highly expanding population areas. While all higher education systems and institutions may do the same and the comparability would also be increased, certain differences are bound to remain.

It is within such a context that the call for "recognizing the difference" between various higher education systems and institutions, when made from the perspective of growing migration, increasing student mobility and making higher education systems and institutions more comparable, as in the European Bologna Process, holds a key position. However, this very call for "recognizing the difference" brings with it not only ways and means of mutual understanding, but it may also lead to new conflicts, which are not just social, economic and cultural, but also of an academic type. The "brain drain–brain gain" discussion is a good illustration of such a conflict. The "recognition of difference" demands then what the Canadian philosopher Charles Taylor[12] calls "the politics of recognition," so specific to our contemporary European diverse societies. However, it is this "politics of recognition" which may bring about a paradigmatic conflict line in our academic worlds. It runs like this: on the one hand, "particularity should be recognized and even fostered," while on the other "the principle of equal respect requires that we treat people in a difference-blind fashion […]."

Such an approach brings to the fore directly and differentially the shaping of national and institutional academic communities. During modern times, universities have mostly been regarded as national symbols and as those organizations that were expected to train the national elites. As academic communities, they were primarily parts of the wider national community and were regarded as their cultural and scientific consciousness. Such a particularity should then be recognized. When expected to face demographic challenges in a globalizing context, all the readily available solutions may however have side effects of denationalization or de-territorialization. This does not mean that their dislocation is envisaged. Being locally placed and even entrenched, they may rather be expected to cross national borders for recruiting students and become de-territorialized demographically, just as they are forced to do so by the universality of knowledge and research and by the information and communication technologies which network them across traditional national boundaries. When they do not act in this way, we may envisage the possibility that either at least some may close their doors because they do not have enough candidates or they merge with others in order to decrease the supply of higher education. Higher education systems and institutions may expand in some countries while in others they may shrink.

The existing numerous reports, papers and books focused on the current demographic shifts, migration flows and life-cycle changes have managed to bring to the fore such important issues of concern. They have highlighted developments, but also the relevant risks and uncertainties. Moreover, the studies are far from

converging. As a matter of fact there are clearly conflicting views. When referring to Europe, such conflicting views take either a "neo-Spenglerian"[13] stand, which
is as apocalyptical as previewing "the imminent collapse
of the Western civilization," or they adopt a view which
takes stock of new economic, social, cultural and political interdependencies specific to today's world. The
neo-Spenglerian views rely heavily on the data that
illustrate increasing cross-border migration flows under
conditions of demographic ageing and low fertility rates
in most European countries. Their story is indeed dramatic: when more than a quarter of Americans are
today from other parts of the world,[14] so that America
can be divided into Anglo-Protestant and Hispanic cultures, when Europe[15] is affected by huge flows of
migrants on the East–West or South–North axis, Western civilization might be considered both sleepily
unaware of the dangers that are emerging within its borders and threatened with the specter of decline or mere
"death."

The opposing view to this apocalyptical perspective
follows an altogether different line of argument. It is
focused on both historical facts and prospective developments. It does not necessarily attempt to write what
the French scholar Jacques Attali would call "*une brève
histoire de l'avenir,*"[16] but rather identifies continuities
and discontinuities, risks and challenges, threats and
dangers, as well as new constructions which are just as
different from past ones as they were induced by them.
To illustrate this approach one might consider mobility
and migration and relate them to demographic shifts
and to higher education openings within and between
individual countries.

2.6. GLOBALIZATION:
ACADEMIC MOBILITY AND DEMOGRAPHIC
MIGRATION RECONSIDERED

Both mobility and migration refer to the spatial movement of individuals. Within nation-states there is occupational and employment mobility, that is those population shifts which are induced by changes in economy and employment due to regional imbalances in the labor market or to the location and development of new production sites. When considering individual movement across national borders, mobility becomes migration and is understood in terms of flows of immigration or emigration. In higher education the terminology has also two value laden meanings. Within the country, student movement, on a smaller or larger scale, is always described in terms of mobility, while between countries, particularly within the EU framework, academic mobility of students, staff or programs is highly regarded and encouraged. Inside one particular country, population mobility, be that for occupational, educational or employment reasons, is more often than not a sign of flexibility and as such is a much desirable way of dealing with spatial imbalances. Between countries the terminology in use is associated with divergent values. Population mobility turns into migration flows and may also include refugees of various sorts, asylum-seekers, economic immigrants, even terrorists or just "foreign trouble-makers," as some would put it. Academic mobility may also be seen in terms of brain drain for some—brain gain for others—if not a mere synonymous brain circulation that fits the universal values inherent to academe.

All this is appropriate to that paradigm which presupposes the existence of those well contained national states that guard their borders and prevent a too large/huge mixing up that would be brought about by an increased mobility of population and capital and cultural values. But when assuming that globalization, understood in terms of increasing mobility and interdependencies due to a "despatialization of the social,"[17] the question is how appropriate this old analytical framework, with all its conceptual ambiguities and conflicting values, may prove to be. When answering such a question, the key word that needs clarification is globalization. This may be understood in terms of the nation-state paradigm. It may thus refer to those interdependencies between national societies that are externally shaped and complemented by international and transnational institutions. Globalization, from this perspective, is nothing else but a sort of growing type of inter- or trans-national phenomenon, which may trouble or indeed threaten state organized national societies. There is, however, another meaning of globalization which refers to that specific reality that would go beyond or would transcend the mere existence of nation-states. This new meaning of globalization would also be related to territoriality and society, but these two should be separated from existing national borders. Under the pressure of globalization, the molding of the social is de-spatialized, just as the space is de-socialized from the national containers. As Ulrich Beck put it, "a territorially fixed image of the social, which for two centuries has captivated and inspired the political, cultural and scientific imagination, is in the course of breaking up."[18] The name of this "breaking up process" is globalization. It thus appears as a new reality and not as a by-product of international relations.

When looking at recent developments in economy,

politics, culture and education, such a reality tends to become obvious. Within higher education, national higher education systems have opted since 1999 to create, through the Bologna Process, a European Higher Education Area which is not meant to add a new European dimension to the already existing national dimension, but rather to "de-territorialize" higher education institutions so as to make them "European players" in an enlarged globally relevant territory. To this one may add the mushrooming of transnational higher education institutions,[19] which are transnational in the sense that they may or may not belong to any national system, that is, they are de-territorialized.

Many universities in Europe want or dream or aspire to escape from their national boundaries by becoming and thus being recognized as firstly European and then global players.[20] Territorial difference is shaped and lived as academic similarity, while academic proximity chooses remote territories and borders. The European Higher Education Area shrinks distances by merging into a single academic space institutions that are spread across vast territories, while in the same institution students and staff may learn and study as if operating in far remote places. Global and local are merged in what Benjamin Barber[21] called "glocal."

The national and global paradigms, when distinguished and accepted, may lead to different approaches to the impact of demographic shifts and migration flows on higher education. For some, domestic demographic decline is compensated by the inflow of migrants and mobile students and staff, while for others this is aggravated by the outflow of workers, students and academics. Such trends may be regarded as a sign of the emerging transnational space of higher education where the impact of demography is de-territorialized and dena-tionalized thus being seen within the context of global-ization. However, such a stand may be challenged by the nation-states, which would strongly defend their histo-rical identity. A paradigmatic conflict, related to the "politics of recognition," is thus at work, and higher education seems to be one of the battlegrounds of glo-balization.

2.7. HIGHER EDUCATION INSTITUTIONS AT A CROSSROADS

Demographic declines, increased migration flows and life-cycle changes compensate each other, and these compensatory mechanisms operate both nationally, regionally and globally. If this is the case, higher educa-tion systems and institutions are differently affected by demographic declines when considering the impact of migration and lifecycle changes. Moreover, there are other factors at work, such as public expenditure and private investments in higher education, labor market developments, staff recruitment and retention, types of study program design and implementation, which may differentiate further.

The key idea is that the type and content of higher education could also influence demography. Though in many European countries there is a need to improve the fertility rate, to slow down the brain drain phenomena or to influence the migration flows, it would be erro-neous to assume that tangible changes in these areas would be possible in the absence of significant structur-al changes in the economy or without accompanying cultural transformations. Upgrading and improving higher education is the key ingredient that may trigger and promote such changes today. Higher education institutions may induce long term changes in the desired directions only when their curricula and the quality of their academic staff, their equity and openness are based on new approaches.

There is no one solution which fits all higher education institutions, because they are only differentially influenced by various factors at work. When designing institutional policies that take account of demographic prospects and their contexts, issues such as the following may be considered:

1. Quality in higher education. Since the emergence of the "quality assurance movement" in higher education in the mid 1990s, the issue of quality has grown in importance, and global, regional, national or institutional policies have been widely promoted. Diversity of approaches has been complemented by converging and even unifying principles and values. Quality assurance and quality evaluation have been also complemented by the growing movement of university ranking at national, regional and global levels. What comes out of such developments is not just an increased confidence in the quality of higher education provision, but also a growing range of hierarchical classifications of higher education institutions, particularly of universities. The former is mostly related to the institutional diversification and multiplication of higher education supply. The latter has more to do with the processes of academic competitiveness between various institutions within and between market blocks. However, both these approaches may lead to a differentiation of universities on the quality scale. Some, very few, have already positioned themselves at the top and struggle to consolidate their positioning, while many others are confronted with the spectrum of constant re-positioning on the higher education market and indeed with that of survival in the context of demographic decline. Mention was made previously of the dynamics of higher education demand in view of changes in the size of age cohorts and in lifecycles. Considering all this, it seems reasonable to assume that when the quality and the prestige of a higher education institution are higher, the impact of the national demographic decline is lower or negligible. However, there are two important extensions of this "rule." One is of a global type and refers to the working of the higher education global market. It is within such a global context that the current *lingua franca* of the academic world, together with the historically shaped prestige of certain universities, bring about an important competitive advantage on their side which can hardly be dismantled. The other extension is represented by the already established academic networks which facilitate a traditional academic mobility of students and staff. Such networks would provide good opportunities for their individual members to better cope with a shrinking demand for higher education. When in a nation-state neither international networking nor global institutions exist, the system may be faced with strong challenges. State interventions may diminish some negative effects, but the migration of the best talents may not be prevented on a large scale. What is likely to emerge is clearly not the result of a simple extrapolation from present structures. Quality and prestige would play a key role in the highly differentiated global market of higher education.

2. Diversification of the higher education institutional landscape. There may be a wide diversification of institutional missions in order to respond to a strong differentiation of individual demands for higher education. Student populations are going to be more diversified in terms of age, culture and ethnicity, learning and professional experience. As individualization is growing,[22] so the demand for higher education is increased, but in a diversifying way. Academic jobs as well as academic staff recruitment and retention are also diversified and based on a sort of "contractual individualization" that differentiates between jobs and salaries. To respond to a diversifying demand and student population, a wide diversification of study programs and teaching/learning provisions is expected. The traditional vertical diversification of programs on the graduate–postgraduate axis is more and more complemented by a horizontal one for addressing a larger variety of student population.

3. New governing and marketing structures and strategies for coping with increasing competition. No higher education institution may adequately cope with the market developments unless it promotes flexible governing structures and active marketing strategies. Transformation is the word of the day. Questions are mounting in this regard: How well adapted to the present challenges facing higher education is the European traditional collegiate model of institutional governance? Is there any need for academic marketing, be it national or transnational? In a world of growing "academic capitalism," competition is not any more just out there in the economic realm. It penetrated the academe and it now demands from it the necessary structural and functional adjustments.

Considering such institutional policy options, as well as others to be later discussed in this volume, a key conclusion can be drawn: faced as they are with new challenges, including those induced by current demographic prospects and globalization, European higher education institutions should implement a wide range of changes, covering almost all their traditional structures and strategies. This is all the more important in the context of the newly emerging type of post-industrial, knowledge based and culturally diverse society in which higher education holds a key position.

Demographic prospects speak about the future and how this may affect, or be affected by, higher education. In dealing with the future, higher education may be approached from at least two perspectives. One approach is based on the assumption that much of what is to come in higher education will follow the route of "more of the same." When this is the case, the future of higher education does not seem to be a problem and is not an issue since the past has already disclosed the future and it is only for the present to help reading what has been disclosed. The other approach may question this progressive line, thus bringing in a wide range of controversies. They are induced by the fact that the old idea of progress seems to be losing its attractiveness.

The challenges to today's universities are multiplying on such a scale that the alternative futures are both pertinent and to-be-questioned. But how much is the future shaped today by the past? One may illustrate an answer to such a question by referring to one of the consequences of the much debated Shanghai ranking.[23] Following its publication, some European governments, for example in the Russian Federation and Germany, and some governments from Asia, such as in China, Pakistan, Thailand, Singapore and South Korea, decided to subsidize the establishment of those elite universities which are to be globally competitive. The envisaged end result is a sort of a multiplied "Harvard University." How this is going to happen is anyone's guess. However, instead of embarking on such a line of guessing, it may be better to look at the future from a different angle. For at least two reasons, we are today more and more fascinated by and interested in predicting the future. One reason is that the idea of progress, launched by the Enlightenment and well preserved ever since, lost most of its attraction and stopped being the measure for everything that comes out in the future. The other reason is more problematic. It stems from the fact that the past is losing its power of determining the present and the future. Distancing ourselves from the past is becoming more important than following on from its achievements. The future, fictitious and non-existent as it is, is more attractive in stimulating the imagination and its corresponding actions. Demographic projections, loaded by numbers and based on countless calculations and scenarios, provide opportunities for evaluating future higher education policies and for comparing them with past achievements and experiences. How reliable demographic projections based on so many assumptions are, is a question that begs for the contextualization of challenges. Changes in higher education are necessary, but basing them on the impact of a single factor may prove to be less acceptable. Higher education is expected again to invent its future even in the contexts of dramatic demographic declines.

NOTES AND REFERENCES

1 Martin Trow, *Problems in the Transition from Elite to Mass Higher Education*, Berkeley CA, Carnegie Commission on Higher Education, 1973.

2 Ronald Inglehart, *Modernization and Postmodernization. Cultural, Economic, and Political Change in 43 Societies*, Princeton, PUP, 1997.

3 Manja Klemencic and Jochen Fried, Demographic Challenges and Future of the Higher Education, *International Higher Education,* No. 47, Spring 2007.

4 Alison Wolf, *Does Education Matter? Myths about Education and Economic Growth*, London, Penguin Books, 2002, p. 173.

5 OECD, *Education at a Glance*, 2006, Paris; *Education at a Glance.* 2007, Paris.

6 Alison Wolf, *op. cit.*, p. 175.

7 UNO, *World Population Ageing*, 2007, New York, United Nations, 2007.

8 Ronald Inglehart, *op. cit.*

9 Ulrich Beck and Elisabeth Beck-Gernsheim, *Individualization. Institutionalized Individualismand its Social and Political Consequences*, London, SAGE Publications, 2001.

10 R. Frank and P. Cook, *The Winner-Take-All Society*, New York, Free Press, 1995.

11 M.S. McPherson and M.O. Schapiro, *An Overview of Trends and Patterns in Participation and Financing in US Higher Education*, Paris, OECD, 1998.

12 Charles Taylor et al., *Multiculturalism. Examining the Politics of Recognition*, Princeton, Princeton University Press, 1994, pp. 25–73.

13 Oswald Spengler, *The Decline of the West*, Oxford, OUP, 1926 (1918). Cf. Patrick Buchanan, *The Death of the West,* New York, St. Martin's, 2002. Samuel Huntington, *Who Are We?* New York, Free Press, 2005.

14 P. Buchanan, *op. cit.*, p. 5.

15 Bruce Bawer, *While Europe Slept*, New York, Doubleday, 2006.

16 Jacques Attali, *Une brève histoire de l'avenir*, Paris, Fayard, 2006.

17 J. Tomlinson, *Globalization and Culture*, Cambridge, Polity Press, 1999.

18 Ulrich Beck, *Power in the Global Age*, Cambridge, Polity Press, 2005.

19 L. Wilson and Lazăr Vlăsceanu, Transnational Education and Recognition of Qualifications, in *Internationalization of Higher Education: An Institutional Perspective*, UNESCO–CEPES, 2000; Peter Scott (ed.), *The Globalization of Higher Education*, SRHE and Open University Press, 1998

20 There has been a surprise to many the oftenly invoked league tables proposed by a Chinese university (see Jan Sadlak and Nian Cai Liu, (eds.), *The World-Class University and Ranking: Aiming Beyond Status*, Bucharest, UNESCO–CEPES, 2007). This has triggered out the debate about "the world-class university" at the same time with the emerging European Higher Education Area.

21 Benjamin Barber, *Jihad vs. McWorld*, New York, Ballantine Books, 1995.

22 Ulrich Beck and Elisabeth Beck-Gernsheim, *op. cit.*

23 Sadlak and Nian Cai (eds.), *op. cit.*, 2007.

PART II

THE NEW WORLD OF HIGHER EDUCATION

CHAPTER 3
University and Development: A Vicious or a Virtuous Circle?

Since the arrival at recent modernity has demonstrated that the knowledge economy characterizes developed countries and represents the direction to which all other countries should orient their development policies, reflections on education have multiplied and begun to take a different form. General assertions, which have an Enlightenment origin associating education either with a metaphoric, benevolent discourse or a sentimental one, saturated with hopes for progressive personal development, have been replaced with economic, social, anthropological or political analyses that instituted education as an essential factor of social, economic and personal development. An explosion of pragmatism, some would say. Oblivion or even betrayal of the past, would say others. Anyway, the change took place not only at the discourse level; it would have meant too little. In fact, education was introduced in the equation of development in order to be analyzed and projected together with other components of society for ensuring an expected economic growth and the associated improvements in the quality of life.

At the same time, universities themselves changed beyond recognition. Terms such as "higher education market," "education services' consumer," "education capital" or "human capital," just to mention a few, are being used more and more insistently. Financially speaking, the emergent higher education market turns ever more global, the OECD valuing it in 1999 (for its member countries) at a minimum of about 30 billion US dollars, which, according to other estimations, would represent about 3% of the total trade in services. Since then its worth in dollar terms has increased significantly. To give only one example, the secondary and tertiary education of a relatively small country, New Zealand, attracted from 1999 to 2003 about 119,000 foreign students[1] who paid taxes amounting to a total of 1.7 billion US dollars. Further, many universities are or intend to become virtual, as student mobility is more and more replaced, by means of information and communication technologies (ICTs), with study programme mobility. Thus, the education market has expanded considerably, at an estimated annual rate of 15%, a figure which makes its present dimensions clear. Traditional educational institutions operate together or in parallel with virtual ones; the boundaries between what is known (from our own experience) and what is revealed to us as new become more and more unstable, blurred or simply invisible. Novelty quickly takes hold of what is already known and apparently modifies it until it makes it unrecognisable.

3.1. IDENTIFYING CONNECTIONS

As this is rather a global trend and not just a simple isolated set of circumstances, it is both natural and necessary to compare a national higher education system with others and see where it is and where it is going. Even more so, for any modern nation, which based its own construction and development on specialists and multiple applications of scientific research, university development or its "crisis" has coincided with an economic growth or a social crisis. In the university, the past and the present are being projected into a dynamic custom-made future, which equally ensures continuity and consecrates change, discovery and creation, or, on the contrary, leads to stagnation and recession. All these are sometimes either amalgamated or sieved out and separated in order to emphasize that particular element which better reveals the distinctive spirit of a certain period. When in this amalgamation some elements seem to prevail over the others, it is quite natural to look for explanations, meaning the identification of motives, causes, and reasons, or to try to understand—that is, to empathically and demonstratively project one's own or other people's experience on a world which reveals itself with the force of the evidence. One can never simply shrug off evidence saying with disarming fatalistic ease "yes, that's it," nor can one venture into a singular Sisyphean attempt to fix the world or escape into another realm hoping to find better answers to one's own questions and desires. Knowledge about the university turns it into an expanding *reflexive university*.

Observing what explanations of societal transitions have so far been put forward, one quickly discovers that too few of them also referred to the university. Old as it is, the university—a place for the inquisitive, both young and old—was left aside, to take care of its own lights and shadows. However, we should admit that many things from outside the university could be better explained if we would patiently and perseveringly consider the way the university itself works. When confronting an economic, social or cultural crisis, instead of looking for explanations and understandings outside the university in order to give account of what is happening in our society of reflexive modernity, we should better look for its roots in the university as well. This would be, in fact, an attempt to reveal the shape and consequences of a vicious university-society circle, which should be maintained almost undisturbed, or, on the contrary, a virtuous circle, which should be created and consolidated. Taking the vicious-circle choice would mean to let the old venerable institution mind its own business, and refuse to see that, in fact, it produces and reproduces not only elites and creations, but also some of the most malign life, acting, and thinking models of a society. Thus, instead of insisting on identifying social and economic factors, which apparently would explain the achievements, and, more importantly, the failures of a society, we end up by questioning the university itself.

The circle invoked above would refer precisely to that undisturbed circuit established in a country like Romania between the university and the outside world in order to generate either high quality outcomes, or a certain consistency of unintended failures.

Anticipating the line of the following demonstration, I should mention that, as far as the state of the university and of the expectations regarding its social and economic impact are concerned, Romania is not totally singular. European Union as a whole and particularly some of its member states show similar developments. Therefore, let us focus on both the EU and one of its recent members.

First an EU example: in March 2000, the European Council adopted one of the most ambitious strategies for developing the European Union as a "knowledge society"—the so-called "Lisbon Strategy" or "Lisbon Agenda."[2] According to this agenda, by 2010, European education and training systems should become "a world-wide reference"[3] for quality and relevance, meaning that Europe would be the first option for students and researchers from the rest of the world. Three years later, at the end of 2003, the progress made towards the accomplishment of this goal was evaluated and a comparison was made with the achievements of the EU's main global competitors. The results cited by the European Commission on 11 November 2003[4] are quite disturbing. During the 1995–2000 period, public investment in training human resources had declined, reaching 4.9% of EU GDP, while private investments were five times higher in the USA (2.2% of GDP in the USA compared with 0.4% in the EU-15), and three times bigger in Japan (1.2%). It was estimated that by 2010, about 80% of newly created jobs would require higher education qualifications, but for the time being only about 23% of men and 20% of women aged 25–64 held higher qualifications, corresponding to a gap of 57–60%. Due to school drop-outs at a relatively early school age, only 75% of people aged 22 had graduated from an upper-secondary school, although the goal established was 85%. Only 10% of the adult population were participating in lifelong learning programs where the proportion should have been, at that stage, 2–3 times higher. Due to the lack of cultural and economic attractiveness, the teaching professions were already in a quantitative deficit, and by 2015, due to the pace of schooling, retirement and natural losses, it is predicted that one million teaching staff would need to be recruited. Given the conditions and mostly the resources made available, this seemed a difficult target to reach.

Considering these data and trends, we can see that the more ambitious the EU objectives, the more unlikely is their achievement if the consecrated level of public and private investments in education or the lack of social prestige of education and teaching professions is maintained. The so called "knowledge society" or economy and the expected or even recommended pace of development require a certain level of education and training, while the latter are situated at a net inferior position; a typical case of a vicious circle that includes society and education.

Similar trends, perhaps even more dramatic, can be observed in Romania. In 2001–2002, the number of students per 1,000 inhabitants was 2,598, while in other similar countries, the number was larger: Slovenia—4,975; Poland—4,641; Estonia—4,437; Bulgaria—2,804; and Republic of Moldova—2,850. The number of universities in Romania increased between 1991 and 2000 more rapidly than did the number of students. As for the future, due to demographic decline effects and stagnations in high-school enrolments or in the number of high-school *Baccalaureate* holders in universities, Romania will probably also witness a decrease in the absolute number of universities and students, and a relative increase in the proportion of students in the total school population per 100,000 inhabitants. Whatever the case, the necessary growth in Romania's student population should definitely be much bigger considering the Europe-wide objectives to be achieved. However, this growth would not be profitable at all if students would not acquire adequate cognitive and professional qualifications. Comments are simply superfluous when we learn that of about 1,000 young Law School graduates, only one is accepted for magistrates training. Is this a structural crisis, a professional (academic) conscience crisis, or both?

The need for breaking the vicious circle in the society-university relationship is thus under double (European and national) pressure. Considering this issue in quantitative terms is important, but nowhere near sufficient. What type of competencies would we like higher education graduates have? What are the skills and personal qualities that future graduates should possess and demonstrate which the knowledge economy/society and trans-national occupational mobility require in the name of competitiveness? How many of the work-life, personal or inter-personal life choices related to the social, economic and cultural world are induced by what is taught/learned in university, and how many external ones are brought in and reproduced inside the university? Such questions clearly concern the links between academic life and the social and professional ones.

The most direct answer at hand is that both are closely connected and reproduce with each other in a descending slope. A "vicious circle" is therefore the term I propose for this persistent, exhaustive and distinct reproduction, maintained by the Romanian academic framework and lifestyle. By affirming this I do not mean to limit myself to the "absolving of sin through confession" formula. On the contrary, I shall commit myself as much as possible to formulating alternatives, hoping that these will animate more prolific imaginations, and more powerful pressures for inventing the much desired "virtuous circle" of another construction.

3.2. MARKET CULTURE AND
ACADEMIC CULTURE

Before looking for alternative formulas, however, let us admit once more that Romania's higher education system is confronting changes and difficulties. On the one hand, after 1991 with the emergence of private universities, the rapid multiplication of both private and public universities and the public acceptance of the tuition fee system, a higher education market began to emerge in Romania. The growing autonomy of public and private universities and the commercialization of education services generated "a market culture" in all universities. The academic knowledge, educational services and adjacent services are now treated as marketable products. The price of these products depends partly not only on their intrinsic value, but on external social factors linked mostly to the characteristics of those who formulate the demand for higher education and their backgrounds. Thus, the university market culture ended up being almost exclusively shaped by the nature of the demand, meaning by factors which are external to the university, and too little by the intrinsic quality of the "products" and services or the essential academic values of the university. The university's "ivory tower" seems to have been demolished and replaced by the exclusive logic of the market. Although based on the autonomy of the institutions it builds, the academic market was and remained heteronymous.

On the other hand, the university has its own academic culture resulting from its rich and conflictual history of production and reproduction of ideas and cognitive and technological innovations. Far from being unique and coherent, the academic culture was always plural and multi-layered with rituals and faiths slightly disconnected, but intensively perpetuated, with practices metaphorical by significance and suggestive by implications. Texts, pretexts, subtexts combined and still are combining in a whole which aspires to a *universitas* vocation. It is about a whole which is not turning into a universal integrating *Gestalt*, as long as it has dissociated into alternative and concurrent cognitive trajectories when speaking about disciplines, and into alternatively integrating and disaggregated individual experiences when speaking about education.

The two cultures themselves—the market one centered on the *exchange value* of knowledge and education, and the academic one associated with the *symbolic value* of the practices, products, rituals and faiths oriented to and induced by the internal and external forces of aggregation and disaggregation—may, in turn, be either convergent or divergent. What is the situation today? To what extent do the "siren songs" of the market culture disturb or strengthen the traditional academic culture of universities? Let us keep in mind that the attribute "traditional" refers in fact to the "modern tradition," meaning the modern university which was consecrated mostly during the nineteenth and the twentieth centuries in the form of the Humboldtian, Napoleonian or Anglo-Saxon models of university. These models had left behind much of the traditional medieval university to which few refer today. Today's university is, as always, linked not only to the forces of the economic market or symbolic goods; it had and still has, beginning with the breaks of the first modernity, a real social and political vocation, a public duty, a constant orientation to national public welfare. History itself has forced it to be this way. At the European level, even from the dawn of its own institutional construction, the university offered a distinct, although limited, basis for the affirmation of the new specific value system which took the form of scholasticism. During the Renaissance period, especially after the Reform and counter-Reform, university autonomy tended to become more relative, so that after the unity of medieval Europe fell apart, it became more and more involved in the construction of the new nation-states. It started to form the elite of the new secular bureaucracies, to offer new "negotiation bridges" between the mercantile cultures and those of the power circles formed around the monarchic courts, to promote new intellectual values and legitimize the new political, religious and still proto-scientific order. After a period of stagnation, which reached its apogee during the Enlightenment era, when truly innovating ideas only by chance found a place in the *alma mater*, the university returned to the forefront in force, with numerous changes specific to the nineteenth century: political changes, focused on the nation-state; intellectual and cultural changes generated by the religious decline; scientific changes associated with the rise of technology; socio-economic changes, based on urbanization and new forms of organization of production. It is only now that what we call "today's universities" have appeared, replicating European types of organization and commitments and assuming distinct functions and roles in the construction of the new nation-state. In the twentieth century, universities asserted their continuity, although their social commitment became even more prominent, either by shaping the knowledge and work division and developing new technologies and cognitive fields, or by their decisive role in transmitting the intellectual, cultural and social capital of the time. In a number of countries, the twentieth century also witnessed, the total subordination of the university to totalitarian ideologies, when its critical vocation registered a fundamental regress, especially in terms of the cultural system of values transmitted and reproduced. Instrumental and ideological values became dominant, while critical thinking fell into recession.

In the twenty-first century, with the development of the knowledge society and economy in some countries, and the fresh memory of loosing their autonomy in other countries, coupled with the strong promotion of instrumental values, the academic culture of the university is once again confronted with the need for questioning both its critical vocation and mediating between the capitalism of the competitive market, the participative ideals of the liberal democracy and a more and more pregnant individualization. Is the university able to build and maintain a "critical distance" between itself and the society within which it functions in order to develop its own system of values—congruent, of course, but also distinct from the larger one of the society—and to propagate it by producing and transmitting knowledge, forming "elites," as well as educating a growing number of the population coming from the most diverse social backgrounds?

To answer such a question would mean, in the first place, to know what type of university we are talking about. For no matter how ostensibly similar would seem the universities of today and yesterday, when superficially looked at, we cannot skirt the fact that compared to the past, higher education institutions are, nowadays, extremely diverse. The term "university" itself is abusively used by institutions which have nothing to do with the term's history or vocations, or even with the least significant organizational characteristics of the venerable institution. Information and communication technologies and the massified demand for higher qualifications have generated organizations which have separated, sometimes irremediably, elite universities from the "Fordist mass production" ones. And this is precisely the kind of seemingly never ending diversification, which makes us question not only the cultures invoked before, but also the idea of the university itself undergoing multiple unexpected transformations. Therefore, we should consider carefully today's university model and compare it with the yesterday's on both the grounds of the commercial market and cultural and humanistic values. Are there any communicative bridges left between the corporate university and the university of traditional humanistic values?

It is such questions that I will address in what follows, hoping that, in this way, we can discover not only the functions of the university today but also what effects its functioning should have on the world around us. First, I shall insist on the university's mode of affirmation, particularly from the perspective of the newly emergent market of higher education and academic qualifications. The language used will be somehow rebarbative, referring to the corporate university and the "education industry". Then, I shall go back to the traditional academic values in the context of recent high modernity and try to see the risks they are confronting, how obsolete they have become or how much alive they still are within the current university ethos.

3.3. A CHANGE OF PARADIGM:
THE "EDUCATION INDUSTRY"
IS EMERGING

Of the new terms being more and more frequently used in projecting and analysing higher education, those of "market," "trade," "industry" or "corporation" have to be mentioned. It is also true that these are the most contested terms in the name of the traditional ideals of the academic world.

The best universities in the world are considered similar to or even assimilated with major corporations which are representative of the knowledge economy and society. Seen as learning and research corporations, universities reproduce, transmit and produce knowledge; they ensure cognitive and technological transfers; sell training services and produce new knowledge and technologies which they test first in production microunits (through "spin off" procedures) or in incubators which function in science parks, eventually launching the successful ones on a larger scale into the real economy. Four criteria are used for judging the success of the corporate university: the quality of the education services; the graduates' professional commitment and competence; research productivity; and economic efficiency. The first and the second criteria are totally academic, the third is academic and economic, while the fourth refers to learning and especially to research productivity, measured by the profits afforded the university. However, it must be admitted that the evaluation of economic efficiency prevails over the first three criteria, although it is profoundly dependent on them. The explanation is quite simple: the performances associated with the first three criteria depend on the available and activated financial resources and, as those coming from public sources are absolutely limited, universities are expected to become corporations centered on generating profit for realizing public goods.

If each corporate university conforms to this model, the result takes naturally the form of an inter-university competition on a more and more comprehensive market. The model was first shaped in the USA, which over four decades ago initiated mass higher education through both public and private universities as well as through a diversity of community colleges, open to the public at large, and institutions that were using information and communication technologies for delivering distance higher education services online. The American model was followed in countries sharing the Anglo-Saxon culture and language (Great Britain, Australia, New Zealand and more recently Ireland). European countries, with their traditional, protective, super-regulated state higher education models, only recently started (about ten years ago) to explore and adopt this new model. They began to increase university autonomy, to professionalize university governance, and to marginalize or even eliminate the collegiate system of governance; in 1999, they initiated, through the Bologna Process[5], the development of the European Higher Education Area as a space of cooperation, but also, or mostly, of intra- and inter-regional university competition, thus integrating themselves into a global higher education market. The latest universities which entered this "global game" were those from South-East Asia, China, Japan and India. Japanese universities, which until recently followed the German Humboldtian model, have now been legally converted into learning and research corporations and invited to compete on the national and global academic market. In 2004, China, through the Shanghai Jiao Tong University, evaluated all performing research universities in the world and made public a league table of the top 500 such institutions. There were no Chinese or European continental universities among the top twenty performing universities (there were, however, two from the UK: Oxford University and Cambridge University). China however, is now planning to invest, during the next ten years, around six billion US dollars in the university that initiated the league table, and similar amounts in another 100 universities in order to make them competitive at a global level and to position them among the top 500 universities of the world. Discussions on the same topic and of a similar approach took place in Germany, and a proposal was made to make some special governmental investments beginning with the 2006–2007 academic year, to build ten highly competitive universities at the global level and/or integrate existing universities and research institutes from the "Max Plank" system, in order to create universities strongly centered on research. These initiatives announced a new academic policy: global from a market perspective; national in terms of promotion. As known, they have already started to take shape and similar approaches and policies are widely spread around in other European and Asian countries. The global reference becomes more and more persistent in the making of a higher education market in which the competition for students, resources, and knowledge/technology performance is the most important principle of evaluation and consecration.

Public funds are still the main funding source for universities, but their relative weight is decreasing constantly, leaving room for private funds mainly from investments in research and only partly constituted from tuition fees paid by students. The national market for public and private funds, in the context of growing academic globalization pressure, is becoming narrower and narrower for the best performing universities and they look for global recruitment of students and staff and for globally relevant research and innovation results. National market seems to be shrinking for such global academic players and it only ensures room for those small sized universities that serve smaller and smaller regions and communities. More and more ground is gained by the trade in education services offered by universities from other countries, either through franchised institutions, branches dislocated from the country of origin, and online courses, or by attracting the best students by offering them scholarships. The corporate university and the competitive higher education market are extending so rapidly and engaging so many resources that the use of the expression "education industry" is not at all inappropriate. However, such developments are promoted by some, suspiciously seen by others, and contested by the representatives of the consecrated university. The university has been turned into a battle field of the diversified academic values and, at the same time, transformations of an unprecedented dynamism are being configured, induced by the aforementioned trends.

3.4. THE CORPORATE UNIVERSITY AND THE "EDUCATION INDUSTRY"

Traditional discourse about the modern university was mostly a combination of terms specific to the national state and the romantic Enlightenment philosophy about man and the transforming power of his reason. The form of this discourse was highly cultural, including some of the most generous humanistic and national ideals, a kind of hymn dedicated by old graduates to their youth and implicitly to the university from which they graduated. Between the discourses built and conveyed inside the university and those about the university, there was an almost perfect correspondence in form, consistency and objectives, as the external reflection about the university was meant to maintain the rhetoric already consecrated inside the university. This probably explains why, if we compare the university with other institutions created around the same historical period, we notice that it remained almost unchanged and, thus, quite singular. For how long it will resist is a question which the present times seems to answer, although attempts to change it also existed before. The world outside the university changed radically and, at the same time, the external discourse *about* the university changed as well, with the language of economic markets becoming dominant. The discourse from inside the university was not left behind. A new rhetoric and new symbols occurred, most of them of an economic and managerial type, but what mostly changed were the structures in which the university teaching, learning and research services are built. *The university is changing; it is going through a transition which changes almost completely the structure and functions that formed its foundations. The emergent knowledge society is consecrating education as one of its representative industries, post-industrial of course, when compared to symbols of the industrial society.* In spite of the reforming efforts made by the end of the eighteenth century and during the nineteenth century by several pragmatic leaders, such as Napoleon in France or Bismarck in Germany, who tried to change the profile of the university in order to make it more powerfully anchored in the constructive realities of the time, the discourse about university and its functions had still remained, even in the nineteenth century, circumscribed by the same terms specific to romantic and humanistic approaches. Only with the beginning of the twentieth century did the changes in knowledge and work division, together with the expansion of the state bureaucracy and European capitalism, and especially the growth of American influences at a time of more and more pronounced global interdependencies, show their influence on the organization and functioning of university studies. These began to change in order to make more room for natural and engineering sciences, which were preparing graduates specific to those professions urgently required by the development of industry and knowledge. The philosophy, theology, mathematics and letters, which used to form the reference core of any older university, began to accept, under the same cupola, study programs in natural sciences, or even gave them supremacy. Soon, study programs in engineering will transform engineering into the most important constructive god of the age. Little by little, the academic culture split into what, during the 1950s, C.P. Snow[6] used to call "the two cultures"—the scientific and the humanistic—with very little communication between the two.

However, the fragmentation of the academic culture was also combined with a transformation of the university which was mainly related to the industrial capitalist organization of work and relationships. Witness of the period and referring to a tendency to "Americanize the

German university," Max Weber, in his famous speech,[7] delivered in 1918 at the University of Munich, reflected on "*Wissenschaft als Beruf*":

> Of late we can observe distinctly that the German universities in the broad fields of science develop in the direction of the American system. The large institutes of medicine and natural science are "state capitalist" enterprises, which cannot be managed without very considerable funds. Here we encounter the same condition that is found wherever capitalist enterprise comes into operation: the "separation of the worker from his means of production." The worker, that is, the assistant, is dependent upon the implements that the state puts at his disposal; hence he is just as dependent upon the head of the institute as it is the employee in a factory upon the management.

This kind of development, which was still shyly warning of the coming changes specific to future periods, was structured at the time around both the Humboldtian model of the university, for which teaching and research were two components inseparable within the academic space, and around the Napoleonian *grands écoles* model, more strongly connected with the requirements of the bureaucratic rationality of the modern state. Still, an important change emerges, which Max Weber accurately observes: the contractual work relationships in the university are similar to those existing in the "state capitalist enterprises". Since then, we can see how the university changed in the same way as the economy and the state bureaucracy of the time; the correspondence between economic and academic capitalism, be it public or private, emerges and evolves over time. Yet, paces vary from one country to another.

In the American area, for instance, changes of the kind mentioned by Weber and other changes of a completely new kind were even more prominent. American universities were already developing specific commercial activities aimed at attracting as many financial resources as possible. In 1906 the President of the University of Illinois was already considering that "business methods" should be applied in university management and, around the same time, the University of Chicago and the University of Pennsylvania initiated "publicity offices" that were publicizing their study programs in order to attract a large number of fee-paying students. These kinds of initiatives and practices made a sociologist of the stature of Thorsten Veblen write a memorandum about the "conduct of universities by businessmen" and condemn the trend. The consequences of these managerial practices in the American academic community were already shaped in that period and Veblen considered it intolerable, even from the perspective of an inevitable and extremely derogatory comparison: "It is one of the unwritten and commonly unspoken commonplaces lying at the root of modern academic policy that the various universities are competitors for the traffic of merchantable instruction in much the same fashion as rival establishments in the retail trade compete for custom."[8] The only way out of this situation, considered as pathological for the classical academic world and described by Veblen as a real "anathema," was to simply remove those university presidents and their bureaucratic entourage who promoted commercial practices that were completely alien to the goals and practices of the traditional universities. But

Veblen's solution was not applied. On the contrary, more and more university leaders tended to behave as "businessmen" trying to increase the number of their "customers" by "trafficking in saleable training."

About one hundred years after Max Weber and Thorsten Veblen made their remarks, we can see that the process initiated during that period in American universities and, more timidly, in the German and in some other European ones, is today evident in such proportions that not only are university institutions strongly anchored to market, trade and corporate relationships, but also the discourse about them and especially their management and governance has changed radically. At the frontier between millenniums, European universities as well as the most powerful universities in the world are tending to transform themselves into a special type of commercial corporations. Two reasons can explain such a transformation initiated one century ago and which is now reaching an apogee.

First, the "knowledge economy," so often mentioned in the political and governance programs of developed countries, and in the analyses made by international organizations, such as the European Commission, the World Bank or the International Monetary Fund, and also in a growing number of sociological and economic works, considers the university as one of the most representative and adapted institutions to its spirit and mission. Knowledge became, within the knowledge economy, the most expensive merchandise and the most important factor of production. It has thus ceased to be seen, within higher education, as only a reflection, contemplation, an explanation, a "symbolic good" or a component of a culture meant to ensure the crystallization of distinctions and identities. Produced, transmitted and still reproduced through traditional academic processes, knowledge is nowadays more and more activated in technological incubators or in quasi-commercial units associated with universities in order to test its economic force within new "knowledge industries," before launching them into knowledge-based large scale industry. Thus, the university, a traditional institution of culture and knowledge, is asserting itself as a distinct type of corporation and is developing not only a market but also a particular kind of "industry" within the current knowledge economy.

Second, in spite of the position it still holds, the university seems to have lost its traditional irrefutable supremacy. Now it is competing with a multitude of "knowledge organizations" which offer education and training services similar to academic ones. In other words, the academic model multiplied and new parallel models, even more linked to the labor market, have emerged. The monopoly of the traditional academic qualifications disappeared. This has been replaced by a real market of higher education qualifications. Behaving in conformity with the traditional model would mean a university will become marginalized. In order to prevent this, the university chooses to adapt, which means it becomes a corporate actor of the market in which it competes with other knowledge organizations.

More and more pressed into becoming a corporation, equally an autonomous and commercial one, the university ends up by behaving as such: it sells education services to students turned into "customers" and "consumers" and changes its organizational and governance structure following the model of industrial corporations in order to propose strategies for marketing, public relations, quality assurance and partnership with industry, even yearning to get listed, when possible, on the stock exchange market (as Phoenix University in the USA does).

Higher education itself, diverse as it is nowadays, is also seen as an "industry" (the most representative industry of the knowledge economy, some would say); as a "service" (next to and together with banking, tourism, health and other services); as part of the economy, which it is not only supplying with the agents it educates and the knowledge it generates, but also producing in a financial form as well as in the form of symbolic goods (in research laboratories) and material goods (in business incubators).

If these are the transformations specific to our times, in what follows, I propose to see whether and to what extent education is an "industry" and how the university behaves on the higher education market as a "corporation" similar, in many respects, to commercial ones.

3.5. IS EDUCATION INDUSTRY A REALITY OR A METAPHOR?

By affirming that higher education, in fact education in general, became an industry I am not trying to simply use or put forward a metaphor. For explaining this, I propose to look first into contemporary economies in order to identify those extended industries which combine a long history of accelerated development with a highly probable chance to further expand in the future. Taking them one by one, we can see that few industries, be they old or new, can be compared with the education industry. The dominant industries of the twentieth century—mining or metallurgy—which supported the other manufacturing industries, especially machine-building, diminished significantly and turned into pale copies of what they used to be. The automobile industry seems today to be affected by overproduction and machine-building is also on the decline. Agriculture, which is more and more productive, cannot conceal the crisis for agricultural workers or farmers who earn much too little compared to the work invested and therefore are leaving the sector in droves, accounting for only two to ten percent of the active labor force in developed countries. With the Internet still in its infancy, large and relatively stable profits are not yet foreseen and the investments made in this field cannot elude the effects induced by the recent bankruptcy of a famous American communications company, an event which is still making many entrepreneurs of the new industry shiver. The media and showbiz industry might be global, rapidly growing and more and more comprehensive but they cannot ignore the way the large American concentration into only two gigantic and global companies are threatening and suffocating more local and limited initiatives. Local companies as well are striving so hard to multiply and compete with each other that it is like watching a battle in which all competitors are fiercely searching for their meteoric destiny. Even the banking and finance industry, once thought to be the driving force of economic change seems to have self-destructed effects, and the form of its reincarnation is unclear. If we admit these kinds of tendencies, all we can do is to remark that, from the numerous existing industries, education, and especially higher education, not only has a long history, but also great prospects for its future development. The knowledge produced, reproduced, transmitted or applied, the technological processes and applied technologies, the people flows and the organizations in which they function are eloquent testimony in this respect.

But where should we look for these kinds of testimonies? Should we concentrate more on education as a whole and consider it in its entirety, regardless of its location—be it in developed or developing countries, south or north, east or west—or should we limit ourselves to Europe, North America and Southern and Eastern Asia in order to explore more carefully its messages and involvements? I propose to limit our analysis to higher education in developed or rapidly developing countries only. We shall notice immediately that, here, the history of education is as long as it is accelerated today, when the institutional expansion and the flows of students and staff seem to have no limits. Educational expansion, in the form of new learning organizations or of the transformations produced in governance and financing, and in the organization and development of their internal processes, is so radical that higher education institutions became unrecognizable even to those who left them not so long ago. Let us say it again that the older history and the current expansion, which gives no sign of coming to an end or even of reaching its peak, are clear evidence, for some, of an "industry" typical of the knowledge society, while for others they represent a betrayal and a distortion of the classical humanistic meaning of education.

What I mean is that, even if we admit that, in the today's world, education is an "industry," we cannot easily get over the fact that, for consistent humanists, an expression like "education industry" could be completely inadequate or even blasphemy, when not used as a metaphor. Seeing the student as a "raw material" during the processing of which knowledge and learning are activated in order to obtain efficient and profitable results, coincides with considering education as an assiduous training within a mechanical-type of organization. From this perspective, there would be eluded precisely the fact that education belongs in the ineffable area of a human construction which is equally unpredictable and demanding. How can we continuously multiply the number of university diplomas, including in domains which, until recently, had no place in the *alma mater*, and yet still be able to accurately distinguish knowledge elites from technology masters? Maybe a certain way of answering this kind of question might coincide, for some, with acceding to the world of the so called "education industry," while to others it would simply mean an unforgivable betrayal of the intrinsic and ineffable spirit of education itself. However, this last reproach could be seen either as a cry from the past of some empty codes, or a call to calming down certain developments which seem to be filled with a kind of insatiable *hubris*. Nevertheless, the force of the reproach is too weak compared to that developing construction which proves more and more imaginative in shape and comprehensive in size. Let us invite the facts to talk.

3.6. PEAKS IN A MAZE OF NUMBERS

Few components of contemporary society can be compared with education in terms of quantitative expansion. But why should we refer to quantitative expansion again? Wouldn't it be more pertinent to invoke the voice of tradition by saying that figures and statistical coefficients are not easy to accept in analyses and discussions about education? Anyway, their validity and veracity would always be questionable and the effects of formal education and even more those of informal education would be measurable and quantifiable only in an exploratory sense. We also know very well that school marks, as quantitative indicators of learning performances, are far from usable as sure predictors of professional performance and even less for life success. However, although they are only indicative and sometimes even distorting, statistical coefficients can help us perceive some of the transformations of education and their effects on its place and economic and social functions. These coefficients illustrate the way a large economy has built itself around and inside education so that the latter would really occupy a priority position in society and especially on the labor market. It is for good reason that politicians invoke it so often and governments formulate policies which are always adapted to the present. Let us then consider a simple estimation. It is known that about a quarter of the population of a developed country is effectively included in some form of schooling. All those attending a school or university have families and relatives who care about them. If we put them together, it would not be an exaggeration at all to say that about three quarters of the population is interested in the daily or strategic meaning and purposes of education. Let us add to all these people the ones involved in lifelong education, or in so called professional development programmes that any self-respecting company or enterprise should implement in order to enter and remain connected to the competition's market games. And finally, let us also take into consideration those who participate in professional-conversion short courses, cultural programmes or even third age universities. What we seem to get is a picture in which education occupies an ever extending position which tends to cover almost the entire population of a country.

We should, however, detach ourselves from this quasi-total demographic comprehension and refer only to those who really are integrated in schools and universities. We should start by looking back at some figures from about ten years ago, before the beginning of the new century, and compare them with those from only twenty-five years ago. We are doing this on purpose, to illustrate how the roots of the present situation go back in time and how what we are doing today is simply to continue those trends in force. In such a short interval, the total number of pupils and students almost doubled. The numbers grew at a stunning pace and continue to do so, as this was shown in the preceding chapter on demography and higher education, and as this will be seen in the following sections.

NOTES AND REFERENCES

1   *The New Zealand International Education Sector Trends from 1999 to 2004* (http://www.educationcounts.govt.nz/__data/assets/pdf_file/0004/14827/nz-ie-trends-report—1999—2004.pdf), Ministry of Education (New Zealand), 2005.

2   *Presidency Conclusions*, Lisbon European Council, 23 and 24 March 2000.

3   *Detailed Work Programme on the Follow-Up of the Objectives of Education and Training Systems in Europe.* (2002/C 142/01), European Council, 2002.

4   *"Education & Training 2010." The Success of the Lisbon Strategy Hinges on Urgent Reforms.* Communication from the Commission. (COM(2003) 685 final), Commission of the European Communities, 2003. /

5 European Commission (http://ec.europa.eu/education/policies/educ/bologna/bologna_en.html)

6 C.P. Snow, *The Masters*, Garden City, N.Y, Doubleday/Anchor Books, 1951.

7 Max Weber, Science as a Vocation, in H.H. Gerth and C. Wright Mills (eds.). *From Max Weber: Essays in Sociology*, London, Routledge & Kegan Paul Ltd, 1979, p. 131.

8 Thorsten Veblen, *The Higher Learning in America: A Memorandum on the Conduct of Universities by Businessmen*, 1918.

CHAPTER 4
Academic Transformation: Continuities and Discontinuities

No matter how entrepreneurial a university might be, it will not be nor will it turn into a business organization. Similarly, the university can no longer simply identify itself with the past, no matter how attractive this might be for some. Between the two extremes, the university must find the right balance and a clear vision. But what should that be? In searching for an answer, let us further reflect on the transformations that the generic university has gone through. The premise of this approach would be that, regardless of how stable the university used to be, one is bound to admit that it has changed and is still changing more rapidly than ever. In order to evaluate today's changes, we need to map out, compare and especially confront these changes with some expectation of their beneficiaries within the environment in which academic institutions function. At the same time, we should know the factors that induce, require or generate changes, how they act and what we could expect. These two approaches, focused respectively on mapping out changes and on generating factors, should really be convergent since one cannot refer to the content of certain changes without referring to the factors that induced them. However, considering existing analyses, it is hard to avoid seeing discrepancies between the two approaches. Changes take place more rapidly than they are analyzed. Factors are more often than not analyzed in isolation, although their actions are as simultaneous as they are convergent.

In general, two assumptions seem to be essential whenever an analysis of higher education is considered. First, the scientific character of these analyses is still in its infancy, and the receptiveness of academics to it is rather low. Thus, a self-maintaining vicious circle is formed with clear negative effects on the developmental dynamics of the academic world. The university has not yet completely adapted to the requirements of our high modernity, which is more and more reflexive. From an academic point of view, it is still in an exploratory and institutionally hesitant stage.

In spite of this somewhat somber image, it must be said that we are not lacking in analytical imagination or organizational creativity when we consistently refer with interest to higher education and its related theories. Recently, the volume of research and works in the field has grown rapidly and, with the transformation of the university, we may expect to witness the emergence of a scientific domain of extremely great interest for the analysis of universities as organizations typical of a knowledge society and economy. In what follows, a set of factors that generate changes in higher education are explored. Finally a typology of changing universities is proposed.

4.1. IDENTIFYING FACTORS
OF CHANGE

The factors to be chosen for explaining changes in higher education should have three characteristics: *centrality* (to be in or to be associated with fundamental constitutive sectors of society); *intensity* (their effects should not be marginal, but forceful enough to orient the establishment of institutions to different directions); *convergence* (the identified factors should have cumulative effects). Further, I shall assume that those factors which meet these selection criteria are the following: (1) the demographic trends and rates of participation in the system; (2) the management and financing of higher education; (3) the organizational alternatives; (4) the creation of cognitive and innovative capital.

Change Factor 1: Demography and university participation rates

The demographic trends and the rates of participation in higher education are not completely convergent. As mentioned, higher education is considered universal when the participation rate reaches 50% of the modal-aged population (18–24). But this relative value, when converted into absolute values, can take different forms according to the share of the population. It is precisely this share that changes, especially in Europe, moving in a direction that raises serious problems not only for universities, but especially for national economic development. In many official documents it was already estimated that in 2030 the active population of the EU member countries will be twenty-one million less, which means there will be twenty million less young people. On the other hand, by 2050, the proportion of people aged over 65 will reach 20%, which makes the dependence rate (number of inactive persons per 100 working people) double from about 24% today to 50% in the future (if there are no changes in pension systems). In a relatively short period, less than 50 years, European demographic decline will be so acute that the prospects for social and economic development are being ques-

tioned, unless of course the prospects of migration in-
flows of young people will not be growing. School and
higher education flows will likewise continuously decrease and young people will bear the responsibility for a
production and productivity able to respond to a higher
dependency rate. At the same time, accelerated technology innovations will more and more often require both
a return to school and university and the introduction of
compulsory lifelong education in order to maintain individual professional competitiveness. Once the "universality" threshold is reached, EU higher education will
have to train less and less young people and probably a
growing number of mature or aged people.

Before drawing any conclusions, we should review the
other available statistical data. In the USA the threshold
for universal higher education was reached about three
decades ago, while in the other OECD countries only by
the beginning of this century could every second young
person expect to study in a higher education institution.
In only ten years, from 1991 to 2001, any 17 year old person came to expect to attend a university study program
for 2.5 years, on average, and the proportion of tertiary
diploma holders increased by 10%. At the same time,
20% of the students were over 30 years old, which means
that besides the traditional young students, a category of
mature students emerged. Such an extension, which is
already established, led to the change of the higher education demographic profile, in conditions in which, in
most OECD countries, the young population has been
decreasing and the aged one increasing. This trend has
profound implications. The demographic decline of the
number of young people leads to an accentuated
decrease in the number of potential young students.
Universities have a reduced pool of younger students,

but they also have the potential to extend towards mature ones, with the development of the social and economic pressure for increasing the weight of lifelong education and improving qualifications. The trend would be for the number of students aged over 30 years to increase as the number of younger students decreases.

Let us consider now the case of Romania. Confronted with the second demographic transition, in conditions of accentuated external emigration and of a decreasing birth rate, in about fifteen years the Romanian population could decrease by around 2.8 million. Moreover, the maintenance of such a trend during the following years would result in a reduction of the Romanian population to 14 million by 2050 (compared to 21.8 million in 2002). These figures were suggested by Prof. Vasile Ghețău who took 2050 as reference year and proposed a "prospective vision of the population of Romania in the twenty-first century"[1] demonstrating that the country is facing a serious "demographic slide" which risks having profound negative consequences on its future social, economic and cultural development. In 2000 the weight of the population aged 0–19 was 25.7%, in 2005 it fell to 23.5% and if forecasts are correct, it will be 20.5% in 2010, 19.7% in 2015 and 14.2% in 2050. Obviously, universities will demographically count on a continuously decreasing number of candidate students recruited at younger ages. In the next ten years, even though the number of high school graduates will grow, in absolute terms, the demographic selection base for universities will decrease. Taking as a reference base (equal to 100) the year 2000, the change of the indicator of school-aged population in 2015 compared to 1990 would be 68 compared to 123 for the group age 5–14 years, 59 compared to 85 for the group age 15–19 years, and 89 compared to 86 for the group age 20–29 years, respectively.

More precisely, if the values of the indices for natality, mortality, average life expectancy, and migration increase for the 2000–2003 period remain constant, then in twenty years from now we would have 2 million less young people aged 15–29 years than today. Today, young people of this age represent 23% of the total population, while in 2025 they will represent only 16.2%. The decrease is truly dramatic. No matter how much the proportion of young people attending university grows in relative terms, as long as the selection base is decreasing, their absolute number cannot increase. Universities could orient themselves to lifelong education programs in order to compensate for such a demographic decline in the number of young population. Such an option would substantially change the academic and institutional profile of universities.

What then are the constitutive tendencies of the demographic factor and their consequences for the university? Let us synthesize them:

i) the EU member countries, including Romania, are confronting a second demographic transition in which the number of young people is continuously decreasing;

ii) the rate of participation in higher education is steadfastly growing;

iii) in spite of the growing rate of participation in higher education, the absolute number of young students will reach a ceiling threshold due to the demographic decline in the number of young people;

iv) technological innovations and the acceleration of changes require, with growing pressure, that adults be constantly reeducated, extending the opportunities for universities;

v) with regard to university training programs, there is a more and more prominent distinction between the services offered to young people (education and training programs), and those offered to adults (retraining and professional development programs);

vi) finally, with the expansion of international migration, universities can offer training programs not only to young people and adults from their own country but also to young and adult foreigners, thus partially loosing their national character and becoming more and more international.

The most important impact of the demographic decline is twofold; on the one hand, we are noticing the necessity for offering training programs for adults, which has a bearing on the elaboration of the curriculum and the organization of learning; on the other hand, the decrease in the weight of potential students, be they young or adults, determines either the institutional association or the merging of certain universities, or the disappearance of others, which, given their lack of noticeable activities, are deprived of any development potential. The competition between universities is sharpening, their institutional profile is changing, the training and re-training offers are multiplying, and the growth in the number of students may lead to a decline in quality. Participation in the knowledge economy also supposes the development of research, especially applied research, and the multiplication of entrepreneurial centers for technological innovation.

Thus, the impact of the demographic changes on universities is quite important. However, there are also other factors at work.

Change Factor 2: Management and financing

The management and financing of higher education have changed and are still changing rapidly, especially as a consequence of the transformations in the social context in which it is functioning. Since the nineteenth century, higher education systems were so designed as to serve the interests of the nation-state. Financing was eminently public, the orientation elitist, and the institutional management, even in conditions of relative university autonomy and observance of academic freedoms, was under state control. The public funds allocated to universities were itemized in expense categories, without any possibility of institutionally transferring funds from one category to another or making expenses which were not approved by the ministerial authority. University governance was of a collegiate type. Rectors, deans and chair holders were elected by their colleagues for exercising limited managerial responsibilities and would often continue their teaching and research activities and limit themselves to chairing meetings focused on academic issues. Major decisions, including those concerning institutional and academic management, were either taken or validated, and often even initiated by others, somewhere in the ministry in charge.

Since 1980s, this model of management and financing has continued to change. The main reference for change is given by the American and Anglo-Saxon universities, and more recently by the Japanese and Australian models, where university autonomy and the weight of private financing sources were and still are much bigger than in Europe. In these areas, the university has become a corporation and the management and financing are of a corporatist type. The data in the following tables serve to illustrate this trend.

In general, in the countries with the biggest annual expenses per student, the weight of private financing sources is substantial. In the USA the percentage of private sources is 60%, in Japan it is over 55%, and in Australia it increased within five years from 35.4% to 49%. In the Scandinavian countries and in France and Germany, the weight of public sources was and continues to remain expensive, while in Great Britain, after an increase in public resources, there followed a tendency to increase private sources by, amongst other things, introducing universal tuition fees.

TABLE 4.1. *Public and private sources of financing higher education*

Country	1995			2000		
	Public sources %	Private sources %	Expenses per student (USD)	Public sources %	Private sources %	Expenses per student (USD)
USA	34.0	66.0	—	33.9	66.0	20,358
Japan	42.0	58.0	9,349	44.9	55.1	10,914
Australia	64.6	35.4	13,084	51.0	49.0	12,854
Great Britain	63.9	36.1	10,572	67.7	32.3	9,657
Spain	74.4	25.6	4,792	74.4	25.6	6,666
Hungary	80.3	19.7	7,656	76.7	23.3	7,024
Czech Republic	71.0	29.0	8,031	85.5	14.5	5,431
France	84.3	15.7	7,411	85.7	14.3	8,373
Germany	92.8	7.2	9,765	91.8	8.2	10,898
Finland	—	—	8,633	97.2	2.8	8,244
Norway	93.6	6.4	14,088	96.2	3.8	13,353
Romania	87.3	12.7	4,415	72.8	27.2	4,875

Source: Education at a Glance: OECD Indicators. Paris, OECD, 2003[2]

As a general trend, in OECD and EU countries the growth of GDP *per capita* was not associated with an increase in public expenses per student but on the contrary, with a decrease. The growth of the student population was not followed by a proportional growth of public resources, even in conditions of an increase in GDP *per capita*.

Similar trends are also shaping research funding. More and more financial resources for research are attracted from the private sector, and higher education does not seem to be substantially participating in this kind of development. Academic research, 59% of which is of a fundamental type, remains prominently financed by the state. However, public funds allocated for research have not increased and the private sector does not seem interested in investing in fundamental research. Therefore, after 2000, academic research was confronted with a need to diversify its financing sources and significantly orient itself towards applied research projects.

In order to identify the impact of financing on university development more clearly, we should relate student education to academic research, on the one hand, and to the weight of public and private financial resources, on the other hand. The dominant orientation of an academic towards teaching or research is being influenced either by his/her own capacities or by institutional incentives, or both. If we assume that the selection of academics is rigorous, based on clear performance criteria, then any member of the teaching staff should already meet the accepted performance competences. This would mean that the choice of an academic to focus on teaching or research would only be influenced by institutional, moral and pecuniary incentives. In other words, if personal

TABLE 4.2. *Percentage of national expenses for research and development by sector*

Country	1981			
	Enterprises	Government	Higher Education	Private non-profit
USA	71.24	12.46	13.16	3.14
Japan	65.96	12.02	17.56	4.46
Australia	25.02	45.11	28.55	1.32
Great Britain	62.96	20.64	13.55	2.85
Spain	45.49	31.57	22.95	—
France	58.92	23.59	16.42	1.07
Germany	68.97	13.44	17.06	0.53
Finland	54.66	22.55	22.24	0.56
EU	62.03	18.8	17.81	1.36
	2000			
USA	75.25	6.8	13.87	4.09
Japan	—	—	—	—
Australia	47.07	23.1	27.07	2.76
Great Britain	65.6	12.17	20.78	1.45
Spain	53.66	15.82	29.62	0.9
France	62.65	17.32	18.75	1.42
Germany	70.33	13.58	16.09	—
Finland	70.91	10.58	17.85	0.67
EU	64.18	13.59	21.35	0.88

Source: OECD. Database on research and development.

benefits (salary, promotion, prestige, etc.) would dominantly result from teaching or research, then the academic would orient him-/herself towards producing those performances associated with one or the other. The option for cumulatively developing performances in both teaching and research is also possible, but in the new academic context it proves more and more limited as inter-institutional competition is growingly intense and demanding, and the financial incentives institutionally allocated tend to be differentiated.

Teaching and research fall under this type of competitive relationship. If the number and diversity of students grows, then the time dedicated by academic staff to teaching inevitably grows as well, and the time invested in research must decrease. When the output of institutional research is diminishing, the prestige of the university suffers as a university is by its nature both a learning and research institution. In order to prevent such consequences, the university may choose to develop one of the two options outlined below.

1) To balance the weight of teaching and research by maintaining a reasonable number of students and engagements in competitive research projects. But what do "a reasonable number" and "a competitive project" mean? Where financing depends on the number of students, the ratio between the costs per student and the number of students should be in reverse proportion, as public resources per student cannot exceed a certain limit, and tuition fees cannot grow without discouraging the demand or attracting students based on their own or their family's income criterion. Consequently, the "reasonability" of the number of students depends, financially, on uncontrollable extra-institutional criteria and is associated with high-risk conditions. The competitiveness of a research project can be considered *in financial terms*, when the resources attracted and made available for applications are relatively large or, *in academic terms*, when the stake of a possible discovery or a funda-

mental demonstration is envisaged, but with risks which are difficult to control and with minimum financial resources. Thus, competitive research projects are either applicative, but less desirable from the perspective of a traditional academic ethos, or fundamental, but less desirable from a financial point of view. This situation cannot be overcome unless universities engage themselves in more applied research projects, in which public beneficiaries are more interested, and which subsidize the education of a smaller number of students not only from public sources but also from private ones (i.e., tuition fees) and from research funds. This option coincides with the change of the traditional academic ethos and of the traditional institutional profile of the university. Current information and data confirm this. Let us consider two examples, one from Romania and another from elsewhere. In Romania, the growth in the number of students was due to an increasing demand for university education and to the tuition fee system introduced both in public and private universities. In order not to discourage the demand for higher education, for over ten years tuition fees remained below the level of the real costs of the education. Universities set low fees and supply low quality full-time education services or online/distance education services of an even lower quality. Tuition fees are of course, below the level of the minimum acceptable requirements. However, fees and costs of higher education per student, as well as the quality of education must be evaluated in comparative terms, through comparison with performances of other universities at a European and global level. Romanian universities have chosen to keep tuition fees and quality of education at a minimum level, and concomitantly increase the number of students and orient the academic ethos mostly towards teaching and learning. The immediate consequences are evident: the productivity of university has research decreased spectacularly, especially in institutions with a great number of students and with substantial extra-budgetary incomes based on a large number of student fees; the quality of learning is rather poor, generating diploma inflation and a scarcity of professional competences on the labor market. The lack of balance between teaching and research is not an attractive option at all and the universities are confronting an acute need for changing their academic ethos and institutional profile.

Let us consider now an example from abroad. The most prestigious universities in the USA or Great Britain are establishing very demanding admission thresholds for students. In spite of the strong competition between candidate students, all of which have outstanding records, such universities do not seek to recruit more of them. On the contrary, they keep the number of students constant. Thus, for the 2004–2005 academic year, the London School of Economics and Political Sciences had about 260 candidates for the sociology program and selected only 10% of them. The tuition fee paid by a foreign student is thirty times higher than the fee paid by a student in Romania and the same can be said about the budgetary allocation per equivalent student. Although they have a great number of excellent candidates, prestige universities do not choose to increase the number of students but to recruit a "reasonable number" of outstanding candidates and concomitantly develop competitive research projects which bring in important funds. Thus, teaching and research reach a balance and complement each other reciprocally.

2) The ratio between teaching and research can be also put in terms of an allocation of "Pareto type efficiency." It is known that, in social and economic terms, an allocation is Pareto efficient when it is not possible to make something or someone better off without making something else or someone else worse off. *Mutatis mutandis*, in a university, it is impossible to allocate more time to teaching without reducing the time allocated to research and its quality. It has been argued that when the time and quality of research increase, so does the quality of teaching. But does it? There are enough examples showing that the academics that are successful in research prefer to reduce the time allocated to teaching or to only work with Master's and Ph.D. candidates, and especially with the best performing of them.

In order to prevent Pareto type efficient allocations of time and resources, which would undermine either the equitable treatment of students or research performance, universities can only choose normative solutions based on a clear vision regarding the mission of the institution. This leads to an institutional stratification of universities whose mission is centered on either research or teaching. A research university selects performing students, develop research projects and raises mainly research funds which also partially subsidize teaching, thus allowing for tuition fees to remain below a level that would discourage demand. A university centered on teaching reduces research and increases the quality of education services for as many students as possible. Until recently, this kind of institutional stratification did not appear to be acceptable to most academic communities. The Humboldtian model of the learning and research university had remained dominant in Europe and is still admired today. However, sustaining this model in the new university context has become criticized both from a financial and academic perspective. Therefore, today's universities are following different development trajectories and are stratifying into a variety of alternatives that meet the diverse requirements of both potential students and research. In economic terms, this normative change is in fact an externality which expresses a "failure" of the emergent and imperfect higher education market. After all, higher education is and must remain a public good and, in the absence of a functional market, the allocation will remain inevitably inefficient. To correct and alleviate this situation would only be possible by stratifying universities and introducing clear criteria for certifying the quality of the academic teaching and research services or for rewarding and stimulating the universities which offer quality services. But this would coincide with a questioning of higher education as a public good.

Funding sources, more precisely their weight and diversification, are not the only factors that influence academic change. Let us consider again the descending tendency of the quantum of public resources in the face of increasing GDP per capita. Why is this happening since in a knowledge economy higher education plays a fundamental part in any development strategy? The answer leads us to education as a whole and to budgetary priorities. In the general context of education, basic education must necessarily be a priority. The lack of basic education, the dropouts or low quality education are strongly associated with poverty, delinquency, social and ecological pollution, economic inefficiency, social exclusion, a fragile democracy and an entire range of other social, cultural and economic evils. In order to counteract this kind of situation with such undesirable social externalities and personal effects, public investments in education cannot be sacrificed in the name of creating a performing elite by means of higher education. Then again, economists have demonstrated that each supplementary year of higher education leads to an average increase in individual income by 10%. However, is it equitable to invest more and more public funds simply to increase the individual incomes of a privileged group? The question is obviously rhetorical. Finally, when considering education as a public good, competing with other social priorities such as health services, environment protection, transport systems and networks, public communications or old aged pensions, the ranking of public priorities becomes even more difficult. In such company, higher education does not seem to be a serious competitor, mainly because, given the impact that a diploma has on individual incomes, its costs must be supported, in different proportions, by different social groups (tax payers, students and their families, corporations).

Therefore, when considering the financial resources of universities, we find the following main trends:

i) public funds made available for higher education do not tend to grow, even when GDP per capita grows, either due to the competition between budgetary priorities or the salary benefits and life style which a university diploma affords to bearer;

ii) private funds must be more and more intensely explored and attracted by universities, so that their weight in institutional budgets becomes more substantial;

iii) as higher education is a special type of public good, the growth in the weight of private funds cannot take place in conditions of a relative and absolute decrease in public resources;

iv) the attraction of public and private resources to universities depends on the type of public policies and the national governance philosophy (exogenous factors) and also on the values of the academic ethos and institutional organization (endogenous factors), that is in the way of promoting incentives for both resource distribution within the university and performance achievement; the proportion between the weight of teaching and research in a university, and implicitly their quality, depend on the type of institutional incentives;

v) the configuration of the financial resources of higher education is correlated with the type of *university government and management*. How this happens we shall see in what follows.

The efficiency criteria for governance, management and public administration have become a priority in contemporary state functioning. Both public and private university management should consistently operate with full transparency, public accountability, efficiency, prospective vision and adaptability to changing requirements. The hierarchical type of line of command and control, which tended to be dominant in some systems of higher education, is disappearing and a new academic managerial and governance structure is emerging. However, mention should be made of the fact that, while there has been a hierarchical line of command when viewed from the Ministry down to the university, at the university level, Faculties and the professors within them practiced a kind of horizontal governance and little management. This meant there was a form of parallel play with one line going vertical and the other horizontal, but without the lines meeting, except in moments of conflict. Yet, such governance structures are slowly and surely replaced by the managerial ones. Such a process is closely related with the ways public funds are appropriated by the institutions and with the configuration of the university teacher's status.

Changes in the system of appropriating financial resources, in conditions of insufficient public funds, would not be possible in the absence of new managerial mechanisms at the level of university governance and administration. Without getting into the details of the changes produced in the system of public governance and management by the end of the last century and the beginning of this one, changes which were strongly influenced by the options of a liberal-type of political and economic philosophy,[3] I will refer to the professional status of academics and its recent configuration.

Unlike the American and Anglo-Saxon system, where academics were traditionally a body of professionals directly recruited by universities, in the European countries they have had an ambiguous status. On the one hand, they were assimilated to public servants, employed and paid by the state, benefiting from all the privileges associated with this position. On the other hand, as professionals, academics benefited from much more independence than the other public servants, holding a kind of monopoly on expertise which gave them certain organizational and political freedoms, even when functioning in an authoritarian-type of regime. These accumulated privileges protected them from both the state and the market. A kind of tacit social contract was instituted so that academics, as professional experts, retained privileges associated with the monopoly of knowledge and expert-type of practices in conditions of disinterestedly serving the public good. They authorized, by the awarding of diplomas, all other specialists and experts, had the last word in expertizing big construction projects, and had the freedom of publishing the results of their own research. Privileges they held protected them from the market games; universities were not looking for profit, as they were more or less generously financed by the state, which was interested in having experts qualified in the fields of development.

More recently, however, the borders between the outside world and the university have moved, as science and technology have strongly penetrated the market or the market has solicited them more and more in order to strengthen the competitiveness of the products and services which constitute the object of the market itself. For instance, before 1980, biology was a fundamental science in which the findings of research conducted by academics were meant for publishing only. The development of research in genetics, molecular biology or other branches of biology along with the application of their results in engineered forms oriented public companies, and especially private ones, to ask for academic expertise in order to increase their profits. By the end of the 1980s, more and more professors in molecular biology began to create spin-off companies,[4] which were selling their products to big companies, or who became members of the advisory boards of the big biotechnological corporations.[5] This happened not only in biology. Physics, the science of materials, optoelectronics, cognitive sciences and many others, be they disciplinary or interdisciplinary, were attracted by the "siren song" of the market and/or began to build a new distinct market themselves. Industry and universities, so separated from each other in the past, started to cooperate more and more closely and build laboratories and enterprises together. Thus, universities as organizations changed and the academics, or at least some of them, began turning into entrepreneurs, developing into a veritable "academic capitalism."[6]

Such a development, combined with the relative decrease of public and growth of private funds, has led to the transformation of universities into a new distinct kind of corporation. Some of them began functioning as for-profit organizations, others distinguished themselves as non-profit organizations, while others remained public but free of the classical state-type management. Public funding became normative (based on funding formulas in which the costs per equivalent student are the main and sometimes the only reference) and global (non-itemized per pre-determined categories of expenses). Academics are employed by a higher education institution based on the funds it has and on its institutional interests, and salaries are often negotiated individually. Finally, a university participates in the qualifications and products market as a corporate organization and, whatever its profile is (for-profit, non-profit or public), the searching for and the increase of profit has become the main goal of its administration. A corporate management can however be of a collegiate type only with the risk of an excessive bureaucracy and reduction of profit. Therefore, the collegiate model of university governance is gradually and definitely being substituted by a corporate one. Austria, Denmark, Norway and the Netherlands universities have already recently adopted versions of the corporate model of governance existing for a long time in the USA, the UK, Japan or Australia; the European Commission and the Council of Europe have initiated pan-European analyses in order to facilitate the extension of the model in other countries of the European Higher Education Area.[7]

The option which seems to be becoming more dominant at the European level consists of combining the collegiate model with the corporate one. Collegiality will remain in academic governance, focused on issues regarding the organization of the curriculum, evaluation of students, selection for financing of research projects, and the recruitment and promotion of academic staff. The corporate model is being applied in the organization of administrative structures, allocation of responsibilities, and selection of staff for governing positions. For instance, the rector becomes what in a corporation is called the "chief executive officer" (CEO) and is accountable to a university council (e.g., a Board of Trustees or a Board of Regents) which includes representatives of the business community, of the Government, and (possibly) of the academics. The rector appoints the vice-rectors, the deans and the heads of departments and organizes the administration so as to serve the implementation of the decisions made. The senate remains the main structure of the collegiate governance; its members are elected by the academics, the size of the representation is reduced to a minimum in order to increase its working and decision-making capacity, and its functions are eminently consultative for the rector.

The rector is selected by the "university council," following not academic but managerial competence criteria. Once appointed, the rector must prove efficiency, transparency and managerial accountability, through both academic and financial profit.[8] University departments are also revenue centers and the non-competitive ones are either closed down or subsidized for a limited period in view of being recuperated. Students are customers or consumers of the services offered, and participants in the collegiate management of the academic departments as well.

The professionalization, in a corporate sense, of university management limits the collegiate management model and practices strictly to the academic domain of curriculum design and research results evaluation, in other words, to the area of academic staff expertise. However, the collegiate management is in its turn evaluated based on results and efficiency criteria. Collegiality remains a form of academic participation and interpersonal relationship between academics. However, its evaluation criteria still hold to efficiency.

Let us now synthesize the trends of the changes associated with university governance and management.

i) as universities become knowledge corporations, their management relies more and more on the corporate managerial model;

ii) the academic collegiality of participation in management is subordinated to criteria of efficiency and professionalization of management;

iii) the application of the professionalized corporate model of university management is associated with changes in the organization and functioning of university departments;

iv) strategic decisions concerning university development are centralized, while departments become 'revenue and performance centers' whose efficiency is being controlled in conditions of freedom of operation; the centrality of the strategic decisions combines with the peripheral freedom of efficient departmental operations;

v) transparency, public accountability, and responsible management are key-values of a corporatist management of efficiency.

The emergent higher education market is still imperfect, the externalities are multiple, and the explorations in the field of university financing and management are prominently oriented towards the corporate model of efficiency. What other influences will market pressures have on universities? Will they remain prevalent, as happens at present, or will they be complemented by those associated with the public mode of traditional management? Will universities continue to change their structures, especially their size, in order to respond to the demands they are confronting, or will they return to the traditional model on which they were founded? Are the institutional concentration through associations and mergers and the stratification by research and teaching universities going to impose themselves, or are we going to witness a further institutional multiplication and diversification? To what extent will some universities have a community or regional profile and others a global one? What kind of relationships will be established between them?

These kinds of questions, together with those referring to financing and management, are far from mere rhetoric. The profile of a higher education system and its component institutions depends on the answers given to these questions. Yet these mainly open the way for universities to adapt to the configuration requirements of modernity and its more reflexive tendencies.

Change Factor 3: Cognitive and innovating capital

Cognitive and innovating capital, more precisely its constitution and expansion, is one of the factors which is most strongly influencing today's organization and functioning of higher education. When referring to the demographic factor and the governance and financing of higher education, we found that their effects were of a diminishing type. This means that, on the one hand, they were inducing a growing competition between universities, and on the other hand, they were tending to generate a reduction in size of the system and institutional range (number of competitive universities) specific to higher education. But cognitive and innovating capital is essential to the development of a knowledge economy, and universities are the most representative institutions for the new development model. Therefore, while the role of cognitive and innovating capital requires the expansion of higher education, demographic trends and a functional financing market generate pressures for reducing it. How are universities adapting to these contradictory pressures? In order to answer this question we should go back to the organization of research within universities and the types of qualifications awarded.

Academic research is confronting a need to redefine not only the proportion between the weights of fundamental and applied research, but also its own productivity. Not so long ago, academic research productivity used to be measured by the number of works published in prestigious journals or by famous publishing houses. More recently, a new indicator has started to gain ground: it is the number of patents of technological innovations, in other words, the number of knowledge products with industrial applicability. Consequently, the testing of a technological innovation in micro-enterprises associated with universities in the form of scientific and technological parks has begun to leave its mark on academic symbolism. In the center of this symbolism lies the cognitive production and at its periphery, the applicative parks of innovation. The problem is that too few universities have a research and innovation capacity adapted to this kind of development. Therefore, companies are developing their own research laboratories or are cooperating with extra-university networks with confirmed innovative capacities. A draining of research efforts and performances from universities towards other structures is rapidly depriving higher education, by means of finances and human resources, of their traditional research possibilities and opportunities on which they formally held a monopoly. The only answer to this situation which universities do have at hand is the doctorate system, where they still hold the monopoly of diplomas and young researchers. However, this will not be lacking in drawbacks either, as long as the feudal form of domination, exercised on the "esquires" (Ph.D. candidates) by the "knights" (professors) who are strongly defending all their privileges, is maintained. European universities are working at present on radically reforming the doctoral study cycle in order to eliminate the feudal–noble traditions and on establishing partnerships with other structures, including industrial ones, for training young researchers. The resistance to change is, however, strong:

the research career is not attractive to young people due to its lack of academic, social and pecuniary incentives; professors argue for the preservation of some of the intellectual property rights and other traditional privileges; costs of equipment and other facilities are often prohibitive; the competition represented by industry and other non-academic research units is too strong for some of the smaller universities. The culture of mobility between university and industry is almost non-existent in most European countries as the separation of the academic world from the rest of the world is maintained, for the time being, by insurmountable obstacles. A Ph.D. candidate is still exclusively prepared for an academic career and the academic codes are too little associated with those of the market or industrial world.

Research and innovation contribute between 25 to 50% to the development of knowledge economy and society; they strongly influence the competitiveness of products and the quality of life, and generate conditions for new professional commitments. And yet, in Europe[9], the number of researchers is 2.5 times less than in the USA or Japan, and in Romania it is three times less than the European average. The difference between the volume of research funds in Europe and the USA is very high. In the 1990s, that volume was five times higher in the USA than in Europe, while in Romania it was ten times smaller than the European average. During the last five years, the European commercial deficit in *high-tech* products rose to about 20 billion euros annually and that of Romania, which seems to reflect the situation existing in other Central and Eastern European countries, to about 2 billion euros. Romania allocates three times less from the public budget for research than the European average, five times less than Finland, and six times less than Sweden. While in the EU about 10% of innovating companies cooperate with universities, in Finland the proportion reaches over 50%, yet in Romania it is under 5%.

And yet, universities remain the most representative institutions of a knowledge society, producing, through the awarding of diplomas, its main agents. When they associate their activities with up-to-date information and communication technologies, the self asserting potential of the universities is even greater. They assure the dissemination and reproduction of knowledge, ensure basic qualifications and offer multiple opportunities for retraining and lifelong education. The problem is, again, one of choice. Will universities commit themselves to keeping the traditional role of research with them or will they give in to competition so that research can be carried out mainly within industrial companies? Will universities establish research partnerships with industry or will they close themselves even more within their academic shell? To what extent will the evolution of intellectual property rights facilitate or threaten the research carried out within universities? Will the Doctorate remain the study cycle which stimulates the development of research within universities or will its importance gradually diminish?

As knowledge, that is cognitive and innovative capital, becomes one of the most important production factors in the knowledge economy, opportunities incomparably greater than those in the past are being opened to universities. The history of opportunities should, however, be converted into one of real action. Contemporary universities are now confronted with such challenges.

Change Factor 4: New Higher Education Providers

New *organizational* alternatives have emerged and are emerging in today's higher education. Some, in fact many, of these organizations call themselves "universities," some others adopt new labels, despite the fact that they are still providers of higher education services. These new providers are highly controversial both in terms of their "novelty" and with reference to quality of provision and their other borderless operations. Controversial as they are, there are many accounts of their inducing important changes in the traditionally constituted field of higher education.

In order to better understand how new higher education providers could and have changed the traditionally constituted field of higher education, let us compare the past with the present. When exploring the past, one may easily see that the number of universities was quite low; so was the number of students. Just like museums, universities used to have an architectural distinction; they were located in metropolitan centers and had associated symbols designed to represent certain national identities, which they were also called to reproduce and develop. Gradually, universities also emerged in other significant regional centers of the nation-state, as did museums and the so called national or university libraries—centers of collective memory and of communication with other cultures. Commuting now to the present and carefully taking a look at the world and at individual nation-states, it is clear that the university configuration is now completely different. Such differences should be further explored by considering four premises.

1) First, let us refer once more to the growing demand for higher education. This is induced by the recent changes in individual life projects, so intensely stimulated by the aspiration of having a better quality of life and higher incomes, both promised and secured by higher education diplomas. The growing demand for higher education is strongly stimulated by the labor market changes which require more and more sophisticated intellectual and professional qualifications.

We have seen before that the effects of a growing demand for higher education is associated with the demographic state of a country. In countries with a numerous population, such as China or India and others from the South Pacific area, the growth in the demand for higher education is so spectacular that national higher education systems, in spite of their own expansion, are struggling to meet it. An Australian study[10] carried out in 2002 predicted that in 2005 the demand for international education (that is for those students who plan to study outside their national systems) would reach 7.2 million international students (studying outside their own countries). This figure was four times higher than in 2000 when there were "only" 1.8 million international students. On the other hand, countries with a national higher education system which was not rapidly and flexibly adapting to the individual and social demand for higher education remained with a significant residual number of young people or adults looking for education services and qualifications providers elsewhere. Take, for instance, the example of Romania, where at the beginning of the 1990s there were not sufficient competitive Master's programs in the field of business administration. Universities had not adapted rapidly enough to an expanding demand from both the labor market and individuals, thus creating a national residual market of demand for Master's programs in business administration (MBAs).

Similar trends also took place in small population countries where universities were insensitive to the supply of the qualifications labor market. In Israel, for instance, by the middle of the 1990s, the government adopted the decision to increase the salaries of civil servants who obtained a new university diploma. With such an incentive, civil servants first assaulted their national universities. But here, they were faced with a set of selection requirements that only a tiny percent of them could satisfy. In addition, most of the educational programs were traditional ones with little relevance to the civil servants' expectations. The consequence was that, in less than two or three years, Israel was simply flooded by educational offers by universities from Great Britain, France, Germany, and Central and Eastern Europe. These foreign non-Israeli universities established their qualification-offering "antennas" in Israel and civil servants made their own move towards universities from foreign countries in order to obtain the much desired diploma which would bring them higher incomes. Hundreds of diplomas issued by foreign universities had then to be nationally recognized, raising the important conflictual phenomenon between local and foreign diplomas. Both locally and foreign awarded diplomas should have had similar effects for their holders, but Israeli universities and authorities doubted the validity of the corresponding quality attributes of foreign diplomas. The problem became an international one and UNESCO and the Council of Europe offered their auspices for analyzing and regulating it.[11]

2) The second premise regards an interesting kind of combination between the traditional prestige of universities and the entrepreneurship of corporations. It is well known how important it is for a company to develop the cognitive and professional qualifications of its personnel in view of keeping and especially strengthening its competitive advantage. But this requires important investments and, initially, companies opted for contracting professional development services for their employees with private specialized firms and especially with universities, recognized as prestigious organizations which already had the relevant expertise, knowledge and adequate technologies.

However, it was often proved that between the costs and the benefits obtained there was a big discrepancy, especially considering the technological, cognitive and trade-mark interests of the investing company. In order to counteract such a disadvantage, to avoid the often expensive externalization of professional development services for their personnel, and to take over the traditionally prestigious symbolism of universities, some of the big companies (e.g., Toyota, Motorola, Microsoft, McDonald's) created their own universities. This is how the *corporate universities* emerged. They do not necessarily expect to be accredited and included in a national system, as they belong to a multinational company anyway, and they issue diplomas whose personal utility is neither necessarily valid nor professionally expected on the entire national or global labor market. Their corporate utility is what is expected, being both important and sufficient. The monopoly on lifelong education or training, which traditionally belonged to the university, was thus dethroned by the new corporate universities.

3) Each time they emerged, new communication technologies changed something in the functioning of the university. Printing, radio, and television are already classical examples, each at their time, generating an adaptation and recovering crisis which proved to be beneficial for university performance. More recently, the computer and the internet have brought facilities incomparably greater than the previous technologies in storing and processing information and in facilitating communication, thus combining many media and operating at ever bigger distances and speeds.

As a consequence of the implementation of these new technologies, libraries are changing, education sources and strategies are being transformed, and communication with students is expanding. Traditional correspondence and distance education became a relic of obsolete past times. They are being replaced by "e-learning" formulas that facilitate real-time interaction between teacher and student during courses, seminars and examinations. Traditional university buildings are being substituted by several rooms with performing computers that offer similar or even better services to an unlimited number of students in the *virtual university* system. Thus, a new university campus is emerging—the virtual one—with a new architecture and organization and a "clientele" that can always be diversified. It is transforming the university into a "learning and knowledge transmitting organization," even though it is not centered on producing knowledge but only on transmitting and reproducing it.

4) As its name suggests, and through the way it organizes knowledge and transcends any kind of borders, the university has a universal *vocation*. International cooperation is one of the intrinsic attributes of the university. Nowadays, this cooperation is changing rapidly. Traditionally, it was based on student and academic staff mobility. More recently though, under the impact of the ICT, traditional mobility is being joined by the mobility of study programs. A student no longer needs to go abroad to attend a study program as the study program can be brought to the student's own home or city. The number of beneficiary students is growing, the qualitative impact can be important, and the competition between universities is also growing and being internationalized. The mobility of study programs has generated a new kind of higher education. *Trans-national or cross-border universities* have emerged, denationalizing higher education systems and universities in a two fold sense. On the one hand, any university, no matter to what national area it belongs, has the chance to (or must) participate in a global higher education area, to explore its advantages and disadvantages, to adapt to the new context or to be, *horribile dictu*, crushed by it. On the other hand, the newly emerged *trans-national or cross-border universities,* which do not belong to any national higher education system, are providing education services to students who can belong to any country.

A global higher education market is thus resulting

within which cooperation can either be of an inter-university type (a number of universities from the same country or from different countries offering joint study programs and qualifications) or of a corporate-university type (universities joining companies, firms or corporations to form consortia or networks together).

When we consider these premises, we find that a global demand and market have taken shape and a diversity of higher education service providers, networks for cooperation and competition, new means of providing education services and benefiting from their advantages have emerged. The higher education organizational alternatives are nowadays more and more numerous, the academic world is rapidly changing and the market is becoming the global framework in which it constitutes itself. In order to better understand the implications of these developments, let us further explore the way they are being built and consider the typology of providers and of study program mobility.

The typology of higher education providers is even more necessary for the evaluation of the new national and global university areas, as they are being characterized by the rapid dynamics of development and by an endless institutional diversity. Let us first make a distinction between the *national higher education area,* which corresponds to a higher education system and includes tertiary education institutions accredited in a country, and the *global higher education area*, which is more diversified as it includes both institutions belonging to the national area and others from outside, which position themselves as global, denationalized institutional "players" or "actors." In this global higher education area we find: commercial companies which offer education services, such as Apollo (USA), Informatics (Singapore), or Aptech (India); corporate universities, such as Toyota, Motorola, or McDonald's; university networks, professional associations and organizations belonging to the publishing and media systems, or the ICT industry. This area also includes a category of "institutions" which are polluting it in force and are unfortunately attracting beneficiaries who pay for higher education diplomas of no value.

These are the so-called *rogue providers* which are not complying even with the most basic standards of academic quality, thus being non-accreditable by the institutions authorized in this respect, and *diploma mills*, which only hold a web page and diplomas nicely fabricated for sale at relatively affordable prices. Who could want a Ph.D. Diploma of Science at Stamford University (note the resemblance with the name of a famous American university!)? It is very simple: you pay a fee of US$ 500–1,000 and quickly receive the respective diploma which any competent body would instantly recognize as fake while a less competent one might admire and recognize the "high qualification" of the holder. Table 4.3. presents this typology in a simple and synthetic form which is further explained below.

We have already been acquainted with some of these providers. They are the public or private higher education institutions (HEIs) which traditionally belong to the national higher education area. Others, however, belong to another category. Let us first eliminate the *rogue providers* and the *diploma mills*, which are functioning under special conditions: (a) when the individual demand for academic qualifications exceeds the instituti-

Categories of providers	Types of providers	Components	Academic Status	Commercial Status
I. National university field	1. Public higher education institutions (HEIs)	Universities Specialized institutes	Accredited Accredited	Non-profit Non-profit
	2. Private HEIs	Universities Specialized institutes	Accredited Accredited	Non/For-profit Non/For-profit
	3. Deceptive HEIs	Fake universities Rogue providers	Accredited by unauthorized institutions Not accredited because of their poor academic quality	For-profit For-profit
II. Global university field	1. Corporate higher education	Corporate universities	Some of them want to get accredited, others are not interested in being accredited	Serve the interests of the Mother Corporation
	2. Networks	Public and/or private universities which are constituted in associations or consortia or are operating individually, within their own international network Public and/or private universities associated with private or public companies forming a private company which offers higher education services	Accredited components Universities are accredited	For-profit or non-profit For-profit
	3. Virtual universities	Specialized study programmes	Accredited	Non/For-profit
	4. Commercial companies	Institutions from publishing, media or ICT systems offering education services and cooperate or not with universities	Accredited or not accredited	For-profit
	5. Diploma mills	Commercial forms	Not accredited	For-profit

onal supply of higher education services and (b) when there exists a number of naïve and less demanding persons for the quality of services they buy, or who merely wish to achieve a maximum symbolic or material profit with the minimum of effort. These fake institutions will continue to exist as long as they are subsidized by specific customers and tolerated by existing legal systems.

The most representative institutions of the global higher education area are the accredited public and private institutions and the commercial companies or the networks they have joined. In order to be able to cope with or indeed to become players on the global higher education market, universities have so far used two mechanisms. The first is a traditional one and consists in attracting paying students from abroad. This mechanism has three major disadvantages:

a) the number of foreign students that can be attracted into international mobility programs is relatively small. Even when significant public investments are made in view of achieving some generous political goals, such as European integration, the proportion of mobile students does not exceed 5% of the entire student population;

b) the number of foreign students varies dramatically, depending on imponderable domestic or international factors. There are two illustrative examples in this respect. After the terrorist attacks in September 2001 and following some anti-migration policies, the number of foreign students in the USA has significantly decreased. After the 1989 and 1990 revolutions, the universities in Central and Eastern European countries lost their attractiveness and the number of foreign students decreased by over 90%;

c) the small number and the variation in the number of international mobile student flows negatively influence the cost recovery for the academic infrastructure. In view of accommodating foreign students, initial investments should be sufficiently high, while the period of recovery and the uncertainty of student flows are working as diminishing factors.

Considering such disadvantages of student mobility, another mechanism was chosen for enhancing both academic and monetary profits: student mobility was substituted by study program mobility. Curricula, manuals, student learning and evaluation methods, and even the teaching staff specific to a study program are transferred from a university from country A in a location that can be a university or a private organization to the service sector in country B. The language of instruction can be the local one, although more often it is delivered in English. Tuition fees are comparable with those from the country of origin of the program. The number of students depends only on demand and can grow as much as possible. Study certificates, including diplomas, are issued by the university from country A and are subject to recognition in country B. This is just one type of program mobility. In other situations the university from country A sets up a branch in country B or even in an independent for-profit institution whose functioning is based on expertise coming from country A.

Each type variations are actually without limits, resulting in an indefinite combinatory range which could sometimes manifest itself in the same country, through inter-university cooperation, or between universities from different countries, in order to offer programs in other countries (Table 4.4).

Such combinations sometimes include public or private companies from the media, ICT or publishing sectors. Together, they offer traditional publications and TV or online systems in order to facilitate teaching and learning processes.

TABLE 4.4. *Combinatory relationships of inter-university cooperation in the global academic area*

U_1 U_2 . . . U_n	Common Programmes within the same country (associations, consortia, etc.)	C C_1 $\_U_{1.1}$ (Country of origin) $\_U_{1.2}$ $\_U_{1.j}$ C_2 $\_U_{2.1}$ $\_U_{2.2}$ $\_U_{2.j}$ $.C_3$ $\_U_{n.1}$ $\_U_{n.2}$ $\_U_{n.j}$	N_1 N_2 N_3	Inter-university networks which offer common programmes for students from the countries of origin of the universities or students from other countries

Note: U – university; C – country of origin; N – inter-university network

Finally, universities and/or commercial companies can set up together a new company for providing higher education services, and this company may function either as a for-profit or non-profit organization. A well known institution, specialized in the analysis of trans-national and cross-border education, *The Observatory of Borderless Higher Education* (OBHE), made an inventory of those companies which offer educational services and programs and which are stock exchange-listed. The OBHE has also developed a *Global Education Index*.[13] The authors identified 49 companies of this kind and grouped them in five categories: traditional ("brick and mortar") institutions, e-learning, IT training, publishing houses, and software and consultancy firms. At the same time, they offered information on their global and net incomes. In order to explore the possibility of evaluating the direct or indirect competitive force of 41 of the 49 companies listed by the *Index,* which belong to the first three categories (traditional, e-learning, IT training), let us review one part of the aforementioned *Index* (Table 4.5).

Twenty three of the companies listed in the *Index* are of a traditional type, thirteen offer e-learning programs, and five offer IT training programs. The most profitable (twenty out of twenty three) are the traditional ones, followed by those specialized in IT training (four out of five), while from the e-learning companies only four out of thirteen are also profitable. Obviously, selling education services became a lucrative business which goes beyond national borders.

However, the most significant fact is that traditional institutions are also the most profitable. The implication would be that when traditional universities adapt themselves to the new context of the education service market, they are more viable and even stronger than the new organizations of the knowledge society or economy. They are the reflexive universities of contemporary modernity, as they are characterized by flexibility and adaptability. Nevertheless, adapting to the context means also bringing about important changes in the institutional organization, governance and management, as well as in initiating and developing cooperation relationships with other universities or commercial companies. The denationalization of traditional universities goes along with their involvement in regional or global projects and generates a global higher education area which sometimes complements and most often de-structures the national higher education area.

TABLE 4.5. *Companies listed in the*
Global Education Index 2003

Country	Company	Category	Net Profit	% Profit
Africa				
South Africa	Advtech	Traditional	5.6	10.47
	Primeserv	Traditional	0.4	0.80
Asia				
Australia	Garratt's Limited	Traditional	−0.7	−11.67
India	Aptech	IT Training	2.3	2.70
	NIIT	IT Training	0.9	0.56
	Tata Infotech	e-learning	6.1	6.60
Malaysia	FSBM Holdings	Traditional	−1.5	−10.14
	Hartford Holdings	Traditional	0.5	13.89
	Inti Universal Holdings	Traditional	8.5	20.05
	SEG International	Traditional	3.7	15.16
	Stanford College Holdings	Traditional	0.6	6.19
Philippines	Centro Escolar University	Traditional	4.5	24.46
	Far East University	Traditional	3	26.09
Singapore	Horizon Education & Techn.	IT Training	−32.9	−411.25
	Informatics Holdings	IT Training	6.8	6.59
	Raffles LaSalle International	Traditional	3.1	28.44
Europe				
UK	BPP Holdings	Traditional	5.3	3.04
	Epic Group	e-learning	1.2	10.43
Ireland	SkillSoft Corporation	e-learning	−284	−279.80
North America				
Canada	Capital Alliance Group	Traditional	−1.5	−29.41
	Serebera Learning Corporation	e-learning	−0.5	−25.00

Country	Company	Category	Net Profit	% Profit
USA	Apollo Group	Traditional	247	18.43
	Career Education Corporation	Traditional	119.2	10.03
	Centra Software	e-learning	−7.9	−18.37
	Click2Learn	e-learning	−6	−20.62
	Concorde Career Colleges	Traditional	6.2	8.30
	Corinthian Colleges	Traditional	65.9	12.74
	DeVry	Traditional	61.1	9.00
	Digital Think	e-learning	−61.3	−145.61
	Docent	e-learning	−10.7	−35.31
	Ecollege	e-learning	0.9	2.44
	Education Management Corporation	Traditional	56.3	8.80
	EVCI Career Colleges	Traditional	2.6	12.87
	Health Stream	e-learning	−3.4	−18.68
	ITT Educational Services	Traditional	58.9	11.26
	New Horizons Worldwide	IT Training	1.4	1.01
	PLATO Learning	e-learning	−1.7	−2.07
	Strayer Education	Traditional	33.7	22.93
	Sylvan Learning Systems	Traditional	46.1	9.75

4.2. IDENTIFYING A NEW TYPOLOGY OF UNIVERSITIES

The effects of the factors of change mentioned above are sometimes convergent and sometimes they seem to be divergent. The convergent and divergent effects may appear in the same institution or in different institutions, thus generating a new typology of universities. On the one hand, one may see how the reference structures and values of the *traditional university* are resisting change, although they are confronting strong contextual pressures for a different configuration. On the other hand, we find that new organizations, which do not hesitate to call themselves "universities," are taking over only some of the constitutive elements of the consecrated universities and practice them so as to get as big financial profits as possible, without worrying too much about the quality of the services they offer and diplomas they award—unless poor quality is affecting their market position. We shall call them *market universities*. Between these two extremes, there is the *transitory or reflexive university*, the one which is slowly but surely distancing itself from the traditional university, is applying only some of the practices of the market university, but, most of all, is symbolizing the risks and uncertainties which the university as knowledge and learning organization is confronting today.

What should we consider are these risks and dangers which are threatening the university as organization, and the uncertainties it has to deal with. Their sources are many-fold and some of them we have already invoked: demographic changes, funding difficulties, globalization, information and communication technologies, market liberalization, new public governance models, challenges of the knowledge economy, emergent types of cooperation and partnership, diversification of education service providers, lifelong education, allocation of intellectual property rights. The list may of course be extended. We prefer, however, to prospect now more carefully the three types of universities in the form of their ideal models, which are not existing as such but are present in more or less simplified versions.

In order to explore this new university typology, I propose a set of dimensions such as:

i) the institutional organization of academic knowledge, of its production (research), transmission and reproduction (teaching, cognitive and technological transfer);

ii) the financial sources and their management;
iii) the students: selection, variety, legitimization;
iv) the academics: selection, relationships, participation in institutional governance;
v) the moral values and their achievement.

I will admit that in each type of university the mentioned dimensions will tend to manifest themselves in distinct forms and variation, as a result of the institutional adjustment to the contexts of change.

4.3. THE TRADITIONAL UNIVERSITY

Hundreds of years old, intensely venerated and carefully preserved, the traditional university is far from heaving exhausted its survival resources. When visiting contemporary universities of a certain age, one may identify certain variations from one to another, but their core reference values, organization and functioning structures, or academic practices are still there.

The organization of knowledge follows the classical academic division by disciplines, well separated and defended by intangible borders. Whenever the issue of setting up a new chair or study programme is raised, the academic values of disciplinary consecration are evoked and a strong argumentation is initiated. The disciplinary borders are more powerfully visualized, the scientific character of knowledge is always questioned, and both the volume and the value of academic community representation and development are carefully analyzed. Academic power takes hold and its force is first of all based on the accumulated tradition and much less on the evaluation of the potential for development. If a new field appears at the periphery of a long established one, its academic acceptability is more probable. But when a new one pretends to be indeed a new disciplinary core, such as the communication sciences, its academic acceptability would have to go through a long academic Golgotha. Even after being accepted, it will be treated as a soft domain whose own semi-scientificity should keep it at the most remote periphery of the academic core.

This academic knowledge division is not singular. It associates itself with other values and principles, such as institutional autonomy and unlimited academic freedoms; teaching and research harmonization – the latter being clearly and definitely prominent; valorization of fundamental, detached from practice, research; and a reduction to a minimum level of any social or community service. The traditional university wants itself committed to its own rules and academic values, without any time or space limits. It establishes its own priorities and paces, any outside interference being treated with suspicion.

From the traditional university perspective, it is the state's duty to finance higher education as a public good, and public generosity cannot have other limits than those established by the university itself. Students must be selected on the basis of their intellectual merits and, as they are young, they must be socialized as future representatives of a knowledge and expertise elite. In this respect, the university, as legitimate depository of national values, will take care of identifying, and especially of developing and promoting them, of comparing them with others in order to specify their originality, uniqueness and perseverance over time and space. Globalist universalism is only a derivative of the universalistic localism.

Academic collegiality is the only method of institutional governance and organization as well as of selection and promotion within the university. Performance is strictly individual, and collegiality creates the base of consecration of a moral authoritarianism which teachers promote with unlimited assiduity.

The Traditional University
- Academism:
  - academic division of knowledge by traditional and strictly separated disciplines;
  - detachment from practice;
  - harmonization of teaching with research and prominence of research;
  - university autonomy and unlimited academic freedoms;
  - minimum of social (community) services;
- Etatist funding:
  - generous (and exclusive) public funding;
  - independence from the market;
- Meritocratic elitism:
  - meritocratic selection of students;
  - exclusive focus on young students;
  - prestige of diplomas and privileges of social recognition;
- Collegiality:
  - collegiate model of performance evaluation;
  - collegiate model of institutional governance;
- Moral authoritarianism and performance's individualism.

4.4. THE MARKET UNIVERSITY

The Market University is an organization that borrowed two of the traditional university functions—teaching and diploma awarding—and submitted them to market games in order to exploit the individual and social demand for higher education and maximize the financial profit. The premises of the emergence and functioning of the market university are:

a) the growing demand for university diplomas and qualifications;
b) the traditional university reticence about quitting the meritocratic elitism and bending the rigidity of the academic division of knowledge;
c) the liberalization of the service market and of the university diplomas as well.

A market university prospects the domains in which the demand for university diplomas is greater, the education costs are minimal and traditional universities are not extending. After identifying market opportunities, it creates an organization which offers the corresponding education services. Research programs are almost non-existent, available knowledge is processed and packed up in manuals, teaching staff is hired from a traditional university, and all these are sold to students in exchange for tuition fees. Student selection is, at least in the initial stage of functioning, a residual one, as it accepts students who do not hold the corresponding qualifications for access to a traditional university. Usually, it relies on a minimum core of permanently employed academic staff around which staff from traditional universities is temporarily mobilized. Knowledge transmission, under the form of either classical ex-cathedra lectures or distance courses distributed through ICT means, is so organized as to ensure the simple cognitive reproduction. Although it presents itself as a non-profit organization, its functioning is totally similar to that of a for-profit one, as it has a single owner and expenses and investments are kept at a minimum level. Governance is of a corporate-managerial type, academic collegiality is quasi-nonexistent, autonomy is private-corporate, and adjustment to the market is a rule and the only principle.

The Market University
- Opportunistic academism centered on the academic qualifications market:
  - study programs in fields with great demand for academic training and minimum operating costs;
  - detachment from research;
  - minimum of academic staff complemented with a borrowed periphery;
  - use of traditional universities as satellites of expertise and personnel;
- Funding relying exclusively on tuition fees;
- Residual selection of students;
- "Academic qualifications market" fundamentalism;
- Poor academic ethics;
- Lack of social services for students or community;
- Detachment from the labor market.

4.5. THE TRANSITORY
OR REFLEXIVE UNIVERSITY

The transitory or reflexive university is more difficult to describe, as the dimensions invoked for characterizing it are taking, in fact, the form of a continuum of variation upon which each kind of change situates itself, at one level or another, in different higher education institutions. Let us however consider some configurations of the most representative dimensions.

The academic division of knowledge still includes traditional disciplines, but in the new context the weights of the liberal arts such as philosophy, letters, history and arts are in decline, hard sciences and traditional engineering sciences are less and less attractive, vocational-type of professional fields (law, engineering, economy, medicine) retain their traditional positions and even attract new structures around them. Classical studies of philology, philosophy or history are barely surviving, thanks to older comprehensive universities. Those which are gaining ground are the new inter-disciplinary fields, be they scientific or vocationally oriented, for example genetic engineering, new materials' science, nanotechnologies, cognitive sciences, communication sciences, public and administrative sciences, European and American cultural studies, environmental studies. New study programs appear in more and more diverse combinations: economics with law and management; electronics with optical sciences; administration with management and private or public affairs; physics with medicine etc.

The new academic division of knowledge is, at the same time, separating and unifying. A university with an unlimited variety of study programs would be, however, unstable, threatened by strong centrifugal movements. Hence the need for asserting the integrating idea of "universal," that is of a university which unifies and offers a counterweight against fragmentation. The rigid borders between disciplines are being replaced by flexible mobile ones, which demarcate not so much isolated islands as archipelagos of knowledge united by multiple links. Student disciplinary identity is much less cultivated. They are being socialized to conditions of identifying cognitive and applicative issues, always extensible and ready to be thoroughly studied. Student progress in academic studies is less and less a way towards a narrow, profound specialization in one discipline and more one of thoroughly studying the management of producing knowledge, operating with relationships between cognitive islands, and prospecting possibilities for practical applications.

Along this dimension's continuum, some universities prefer to position themselves on the side of the traditional academic division, while others are rapidly experimenting with new disciplinary combinations. The first are stable until ossification, the latter are kept in a chaos of study program multiplication limited only by a lack of funds. As the transitory university is also reflexive, it is still constructing itself on this dimension, and the success recipe has not yet been written. What remains are the authorities' unsuccessful attempts to regulate "lists of specializations" or "study fields," which are distinct evidence of the transitory university's instability.

The transitory university is more and more widely oscillating between teaching and research. The Humboldtian harmonization, in which only teaching based on research is strictly speaking academic, is considered to be, for the moment, the European model of the university. In the Anglo-Saxon or American area the option of separating teaching from research in universities is more and more accepted and desired; therefore, universities exclusively centered on quality teaching are not necessarily inferior to those which are focused on research and accept teaching only as another formative exercise for research.

Some misunderstandings regarding the institutional choices for a teaching or research profile could be originated in meanings usually associated with research. Where does genuine research start and where does it stop, is a question more and more frequently asked, but which has not yet received a univocal answer. For some, classical academic scholarship, which consists in organizing and reorganizing existing knowledge, in searching for hidden meanings or in adding new ones, would be part of research. So would the analyses of applicative effects, which, when referring to the empirical universe, would discover new technical and technological utility projects. For others, research is eminently creative, discovering, and innovating. If all of these three interpretations (scholastic, simply applicative and innovating) are considered to be defining for research, then it must be also accepted that any university should combine teaching and research. After all, the designing of a curriculum or a university textbook is based on the same type of scholastic analysis, on the research of the knowledge produced in view of transmitting and reproducing it through teaching.

But if the meaning of research is the hard one, the one of discovering, innovating and inventing new things, then it would be difficult to admit that research is carried out in any university. Scientific conferences, symposia and others of the kind appear as simple academic games with knowledge already produced but not at all as forms of manifestation of genuine scientific research. As we have already seen, the "Pareto efficiency" optimum of time and responsibility allocation will necessarily require the sacrification of one of the two components in favor of achieving the quality of the other. For the time being, the transitory university is either hiding under the traditional academic hypocrisy and pretends that both teaching and research are necessarily to be undertaken, when in fact it is only teaching which the dominant activity is, or it firmly opts out for selecting students in an elitist manner, and subordinating teaching to research. The prestige is clearly associated with the latter and the diploma market overvalues those issued by research universities. Anyway, the relationships between transitory universities and research are ambiguous and they may remain as such for a long time.

University autonomy and academic freedoms are far from loosing their relevance. The issues which are now keeping them as transitory universities are the intellectual property rights and the collegial relationships between academics. Sharing property rights between researcher, funder and university has not yet reached that legal and financial formula that would satisfy all parties. The researcher wants to have the freedom to publish and the right to obtain part of the revenues brought in by his/her own discovery or innovation; the funder wants to hold the exclusive monopoly, even for a limited period, of the newly produced knowledge and innovation, which, in fact, he/she has financed; and the university, based on the facilities it has offered, wants to participate in the symbolic and financial revenues which its researcher has produced. How can we balance the forces and interests of these individual and collective actors without disadvantaging any of them? It is hard to answer this question, as research is increasingly expensive, as more and more researchers are also entrepreneurs eager to supplement their incomes, and universities, in the absence of funds brought in by research, are constantly becoming poorer.

University autonomy is equally affected by academic collegiality. This is sometimes transformed into an academic oligarchy in which the power holders select, dictate, and unscrupulously follow their own interests. The oligarchy is constituted within universities around prestigious journals, in the relationship with the funders, and in getting access to or being confirmed in prestigious academic positions. It takes the form of a prestige and influence network, is impenetrable, non-transparent, and omnipresent. It casts privileges and (punitive) sanctions, defends the entrance doors, and opens the ones to exclusion. Built in the name of university autonomy, collegiality and freedom, the university oligarchy is like an octopus which grabs or lets go according to its own rules and principles. When it associates itself with an age ideology, be it young or gerontocratic, the struggle for academic power is also one between generations which are no longer succeeding each other naturally, but excluding each other reciprocally. The transitory university is thus confronted with the need for a new construct of university autonomy, academic freedoms, and intellectual property rights.

As a place for values' confrontation, no matter how opposed these are, and of rational reconciliation, the transitory university is called to, and often succeeds in building individual citizenship and social civism, and offers ground for the development and guiding of social construction. Therefore, the services it offers to the community or the city are as necessary as they are desired. The nation-states' universities have already identified themselves with such a *civitas* spirit. The transitory universities, multiplied and varied as they are, are still searching for the most adequate references to the services they can offer. Between global and local, the range is so comprehensive that any university has the chance to choose. The problem is that opportunities and possibilities to opt for innovations are limited.

Therefore, only a small number of universities would have the chance to manifest globally, some more will be national, and the most numerous would remain regional or local; there will be national systems without any global university; there will be an academic mobility area within which students and staff will move according to their performances; in general, there will be a spatial and academic repositioning of universities. There then emerges a new stratification of universities which, until recently, could not have been perceived. In Europe, for instance, there is already in the making a stratification of "European" universities, meaning regional universities with a global vocation, national universities, and local or community universities, which are mainly serving the interests of a limited geographic area, with no chances of moving beyond this narrow intra-national area.

With regard to funding, the transitory university is reducing the dependence on public resources; it is diversifying and stressing the importance of private sources, including those from tuition fees, for both research and teaching. Although the option for the non-profit model will prevail, the transitory university tends to detach itself from the etatist public system and assert itself as a teaching and research corporation which acts entrepreneurially and cultivates a value loaded cosmopolitism of an extended (global) civism type. Students of a transitory university will cease being only representatives of a youth meritocratic elitism. Such universities will opt for age and profession heterogeneity, although some of them will remain elitist and others will situate themselves, on the academic performance continuum, on those positions on which they have built their prestige.

In Table 4.6 a presentation of the various options for transitory universities together with their instances of reference is schematically outlined.

Following on from the prospective or actual changes in the transitory university, one may see that this is searching for a profile which is far from being unique. The linear modernization of traditional universities is being substituted by a diversity of options. Out of the combination of various options a range of alternative and concurrent institutional profiles would result. Each university builds its own profile, affirms its own distinction, and positions itself in the academic stratifications which emerge for a period and change in another. The stratification and prestige games will be numerous, always built and rebuilt, so that each university will try to define its own distinction through a permanently changing institutional profiling. In this attempt, it will be confronted with the dilemmas associated with various possible and probable options and with more or less predictable risks.

TABLE 4.6. The zigzag of the reflexive university evolution as transitory universit

Instances	State	Market	Civil Society		
Transformations	Destructured Etatism	Emergent Corporatism	Global, regional, national or local Civism		
Options Institutional Profiling	The state will promote incentive policies and undermine the state dependence of universities	Universities will become knowledge and learning corporations, will professionalize their own management and will keep academics' participation in governance at a consultative level	Universities will opt for a comopolitism of their social and civic services' values, combining global-reference values with national and local-reference ones. Moral authoritarianism will be eliminated and cosmopolite values will be emancipated (through courses, publications etc.) Options and combinations generating a distinct type of university profile		
Instances	Knowledge and Innovation	Academics		Students	
Transformations	Academic Entrepreneurship	Disciplinary and especially inter disciplinary organization by problems of teaching and research	Trans-institutional Networks	Diversification by age and performances of student population	
Options Institutional Profiling	Orientation towards profit, maximization of the academic and financial profits of universities and academics, transformation of each university component into a "profit and revenue center" with the elimination of those which are academically and financially inefficient	Performance-based academic mobility within homogeneous networks of interests and performances	Performance-based academic mobility within homogeneous networks of interests and performances	Meritocratic elitism versus student heterogeneity	

4.6. FACING DILEMMAS: THE
NEED TO CHOOSE

The existing analyses of the immediate future of the university[14] have formulated a diversity of questions and identified a number of challenges. They have clearly demonstrated how difficult the elaboration of policies regarding the future development of higher education has become. However, despite all the difficulties, nobody may propose an integrated agenda of current higher education policies without answering at least some of the key-questions regarding the future options and challenges confronting the contemporary university. Whatever the stand, a set of five dilemmas seem to hold the key positions, set out here as sharply contrasting choices:

- *Higher education funding:* to what extent is higher education either a public good, whose funding should be eminently public, or another type of good, whose funding should be made from public and private funds, including tuition fees?
- *University extension:* should universities select students according to their academic merits (meritocratic selection) or should they be open to young and adult persons, according to the demand for academic qualifications?
- *Academic profile:* when defining their own academic profile, how should universities opt for and balance the weight of teaching and research?
- *University governance:* should the collegiate model be preserved or should it be replaced by a professionalized management?
- *University ecology:* is the university, through its vocation and value practice, a global, regional, national, or a local institution?

The dominant rhetoric of our high modernity is that of interrogation. Navigating through the above mentioned dilemmas would only be possible by extending and developing our knowledge about universities. This is the only way out, because this helps to substantiate the options and allow a particular university to choose a distinct trajectory for itself. The times when all universities were so much alike as to assume a unique identity have been left behind. From now on, we will have to deal with the multiplication of university identities and trajectories. As for the state's regulation function, it will be reduced to managing quality assurance standards in teaching, learning, and research, and assuming the public responsibility of competitive funding.

Whatever the approaches taken or decisions made, it seems imperative that universities dedicated to inquiry and analysis become reflective about themselves. The view of universities as places that simply grow as the accumulation of knowledge grows, as simply collections of academic and professional faculties whose largely independent activities are all that really matter has become a set anachronisms. Left unexamined, they threaten the very existence of the modern university. In a world in which reflexivity is essential, the university has an obligation to be reflexive about itself.

NOTES AND REFERENCES

1 Vasile V. Ghețău, *Anul 2050. Va ajunge populația României la mai puțin de 16 milioane de locuitori?* [The Year 2050. Will the Population of Romania Fall to Less than 16 Million Inhabitants?], București, Academia Română, 2004.
2 For Romania, estimations are based on data offered by the *Statistical Yearbook, 2006.*

3 Joseph Stiglitz, *Globalization and its Discontents*, London, Allen Lane/Penguin Press, 2002. See also: Pierre Bourdieu, *Acts of Resistance: Against the New Myths of Our Time.* Oxford, Polity Press, 1998; D. Owen (ed.), *Sociology after Postmodernism*, London, Sage, 1997; S. Mulhall and A. Swift, *Liberals and Communitarians.* Oxford, Blackwell, 1992.

4 Small companies which were producing at reduced industrial scale, products resulting from university laboratories.

5 S. Krimsky, *Biotechnics and Society: the Rise of Industrial Genetics*, New York, Praeger, 1991.

6 S. Slaughter and L.L. Leslie, *Academic capitalism: Politics, Policies and the Entrepreneurial University,* Baltimore, MD: The Johns Hopkins University Press, 1999.

7 Commission of the European Communities, *Mobilizing the Brainpower of Europe: Enabling Universities to Make their Full Contribution to the Lisbon Strategy.* Communication from the Commission, COM (2005) 152 Final.

8 The academic profit may be expressed in terms of the quality of awarded qualifications and quantum of knowledge and newly produced technology, validated by the academic and financial market.

9 Commission of the European Communities, *Towards a European Research Area.* Communication from the Commission, COM (2000) 6.

10 IDP Education Australia, *Global Student Mobility 2025*, Canberra, IDP Education Australia, 2002.

11 L. Wilson and L. Vlăsceanu, Transnational Education and Recognition of Qualifications, in *Internationalization of Higher Education: An Institutional Perspective,* Bucharest, UNESCO–CEPES, 2000.

12 For reason of comparison, see also: J. Knight, *Cross-border Education in a Trade Environment: Complexities and Policy Implications.* Background Report [for the] Workshop on Implications of WTO/GATS for Higher Education in Africa, African Association of Universities, Accra, Ghana, April 27–29, 2004; S.Z. Cunningham et al., *The Business of Borderless Education*, Canberra, Australian Department of Education, OECD, 2000; *Internationalization and Trade of Higher Education. Challenges and Opportunities.* Paris, OECD, 2004.

13 R. Garrett and D. MacLean, *The Global Education Index 2004*, Part 1: Public Companies–Share Price & Financial Results. Part 2: Public Companies–relationships with higher education. London, The Observatory on Borderless Higher Education, 2004.

14 S. Vincent-Lancrin, Building Future Scenarios for Universities and Higher Education. An International approach. *Policy Futures in Education*, vol. 2, No. 2, 2004; J. Enders et al, *The 20th Anniversary CHEPS Scenarios—The European higher education and research landscape 2020*, Enschede, CHEPS. University of Twente, 2004.

Index